nihongo notes 7
situational japanese 2

by osamu mizutani
nobuko mizutani

The Japan Times

First edition:　May 1986
Third printing:　October 1989

Jacket design by Koji Detake

ISBN4-7890-0306-x

Published by The Japan Times, Ltd.
5-4, Shibaura 4-chome, Minato-ku, Tokyo 108, Japan

Printed in Japan

FOREWORD

This book is a compilation of 74 columns appearing in *The Japan Times* from September 16, 1984 to February 9, 1986. (The preceding 424 columns have been published as *Nihongo Notes 1, 2, 3, 4, 5* and *6*. Nihongo Notes 6 is entitled *Situational Japanese 1*.)

It is a great pleasure for us to be able to publish another volume, and we are very grateful for your continued interest. We hope that you will enjoy reading this volume and that it will help you to understand the Japanese language more fully.

In this volume, we have attempted to explain, among other things, how the Japanese talk in familiar conversation, how men's and women's speech differ, how pronunciation changes in rapid speech, and how the topic is indicated in Japanese sentences. Throughout, we have concentrated on actual speech patterns used in daily life.

We sould like to acknowledge the help of Janet Ashby, who checked the English for these columns and offered valuable suggestions just as she did for the preceding five volumes.

May, 1986
Osamu and Nobuko Mizutani

CONTENTS

Note Concerning Romanization

The romanization used in this book (as well as in *An Introduction to Modern Japanese*) is based on the Hepburn system with the following modifications.

1. When the same vowel occurs consecutively, the letter is repeated rather than using the "-" mark.

    ex. *Tookyoo*　　(instead of *Tōkyō*)

2. The sound indicated by the hiragana ん is written with "*n*" regardless of what sound follows it.

    ex. *shinbun*　　(instead of *shimbun*)
    ex. *shinpai*　　(instead of *shimpai*)

The words connected with hyphens are pronounced as one unit.

    ex. *genki-desu*
    ex. *Soo-desu-ne*

Sonna vs. *soo-yuu*

Yesterday afternoon Mr. Lerner overheard Miss Yoshida answering a telephone call from someone, obviously a stranger. She listened for a while and said:

Soo-yuu koto-wa kochira-dewa yatte-orimasen-node . . .
(We do not do that sort of thing here.)

He understood that the speaker had been asking her about something inapplicable to them, and he realized that he did not use *soo-yuu* himself; he wondered if *sonna* could have been used instead.

*   *   *

Expressions ending in *-nna,* namely *konna, son-na, anna* and *donna,* are said to come from *kono yoona* (like this), *sono yoona* (like that), etc., while expressions ending with *-yuu* like *koo-yuu, soo-yuu, aa-yuu,* and *doo-yuu* originally mean "called this way," "called that way," etc. The two sets of expressions are used in similar ways, but there are some differences between them.

One difference is that the *-nna* expressions can be emotional or deprecatory. You can say either

Sonna koto-wa shitaku arimasen.
そんな ことは したく ありません。

or

Soo-yuu koto-wa shitaku arimasen.
そういう ことは したく ありません。

to mean "I don't want to do that sort of thing," but the first one sounds more emotional. If someone says

8

Anna hito . . .

he definitely devaluates the person in question.

Another difference is that while the *-nna* expressions involve subjective descriptions of someone or something, the *-yuu* expressions are used for factual information. Namely, if you ask about someone saying

> *Donna hito-desu-ka.*
> どんな　人ですか。
> (What kind of person is he/she?)

the answer will be something like

> *Shinsetsuna hito-desu.*
> (He /She is a kind person.)
> *See-ga takakute yaseta hito-desu.*
> (He/She is tall and thin.)

On the other hand, if the question is

> *Doo-yuu hito-desu-ka.*
> どういう　人ですか。

the answer will be something like

> *Ginkoo-ni tsutomete-iru hito-desu.*
> (He/She works at a bank.)
> *Daigaku-jidai-no tomodachi-desu.*
> (He/She is a friend of mine from my college days.)

Expressions used to attract someone's attention

Yesterday afternoon Mr. Lerner, Mr. Takada and Miss Yoshida were having coffee in the lounge. A group of young women came in and noticed Miss Yoshida, who was sitting with her back to them. One of the women called to her saying

Nee.
ねえ。
(Hey.)

and she immediately turned around.

Mr. Lerner had noticed that there are many words to call someone's attention, and thought this must be the shortest one; he wondered if *yoo* could also be used.

*   *   *

To attract someone's attention, you can use his name as in

Yamada-san!
山田さん！

or start off with other words as in

Anoo, Yamada-san.
あのう、山田さん。

The young women at Mr. Lerner's office could have attracted Miss Yoshida's attention by saying

Ano-ne, Yoshida-san.
or
Nee, Yoshida-san.

10

Very often names are left out when there is no particular need to distinguish one person from others present. In the case of the women calling to Miss Yoshida, they did not have to say *Yoshida-san* because *nee* is a familiar term and the two men would not be addressed with this term. *Ano-ne* and *Nee* are often used to attract someone's attention between good friends and family members. *Yoo* can also be used by men, but this is rather rude.

When trying to attract a stranger's attention, you cannot use his name so you should use *moshi-moshi* or *anoo*. These two can be used in polite situations. *Ano-ne* sounds familiar.

Some people, especially elderly women, use *chotto* to younger people; this sounds familiar. *Oi* sounds rude; it can be used between male friends, but it is not used to politely attract a stranger's attention. *Oi* reminds many older Japanese of the days when policemen used to speak to people quite rudely, and it also sounds like an old-fashioned husband attracting his wife's attention.

A use of phrases ending with ...*te*

Yesterday afternoon Mr. Lerner wanted to ask Miss Yoshida for some help, and said

Isogashikute, tetsudatte-kuremasen-ka.

meaning "I'm very busy. Could you help me?" She said she would, but she remarked that this sentence sounded wrong. She thought he should have said

Isogashii-node, tetsudatte-kuremasen-ka.
(*lit.* I'm busy, so could you help me?)

Mr. Lerner had thought phrases ending with ...*te* express a reason so that he could use *Isogashikute* to mean "I'm busy, so . . ."

*   *   *

Phrases ending with ...*te* are often used for indicating a reason as in

Atsukute, shigoto-ga dekimasen.
暑くて、仕事が　できません。
(It's so hot that I can't work.)
Okane-ga nakute, kaemasen.
(I have no money, so I can't buy it.)

They are often used for expressing gratitude or apology as in

Osoku natte sumimasen.
おそく　なって　すみません。
(I'm sorry I'm late.)
Iroiro oshiete-itadaite, arigatoo-gozaimashita.
(Thank you very much for your kind instructions.)

12

But phrases ending with . . .*te* indicating a reason cannot be used with a request. In other words, if the first part of the sentence ending with . . .*te* is a statement, what follows must also be a statement. It is all right to connect

Okane-ga nakute (I don't have money and) and
　　kaemasen. (I can't buy it.)

because both phrases are statements. You cannot connect *okane-ga nakute* and *kashite-kudasai* (please lend me some) because the first is a statement and the second is a request.

When you indicate a reason and then ask for something, you have to end the first phrase with such expressions as *node, kara* or *n-desu-kedo*. Mr. Lerner should have used either *Isogashii-n-desu-kedo* or *Isogashii-node* before *tetsudatte-kuremasen-ka.*

The use of *sumu* (to suffice)

Yesterday afternoon Miss Yoshida reported that Mr. Kato had taken ill and been hospitalized. When questioned further, she said

Shujutsu-wa shinaide sunda soo-desu.
手術は しないで すんだ そうです。

Mr. Lerner understood that Mr. Kato did not have to have an operation, but he did not quite understand the expression . . . *naide sunda.*

*   *   *

The word *sumu* is used in several ways. In one usage, it means that something is finished as in

Shigoto-wa moo sumimashita.
(The work is finished.)

It also means "to be sufficient," "to suffice," as in

Kinoo-no paatii-wa ichiman-en-de sunda.
(I had to spend only 10,000 yen for yesterday's party — *lit.* With 10,000 yen it was sufficient for yesterday's party.)

Kono-goro-no koto-da-kara, ie-o ikken kariru-to shitara, juuman-en-ja sumanai-deshoo.
(Since prices are as they are today, renting a house will cost more than 100,000 yen — *lit.* . . . 100,000 yen will not be sufficient.)

The common expression *Sumimasen* (I am sorry) can be paraphrased as "My apology will not be enough to justify my rudeness."

This verb is often used in the set expression . . .

naide/nakute sumu, which means "do not have to
. . ." or "be spared . . . ing" as in

*Teate-ga hayakatta-node, shujutsu-o shinaide
sumimashita.*
(Since he received medical treatment early, he
did not have to have an operation — *lit.* . . . without
performing an operation it was sufficient.)

*Kondo-no shiken-wa yasashisoo-da-kara, amari
benkyoo-shinakute sumu-daroo.*
(The examination this time sounds like it will
be easy, so I won't have to study hard.)

*Hitori-gurashi-da-kara, hito-ni ki-o tsukawanaide
sumimasu.*
(Since I live alone, I don't have to worry about
getting along with anyone else — namely, I'm
spared of the consideration which would be
necessary if I lived with other people.)

Expressions for accepting an offer

Yesterday afternoon when Mr. Lerner was talking with Mr. Takada, his colleague, Miss Yoshida brought a pack of documents he had asked her to arrange for a conference. After Mr. Takada looked through it and said it was okay, she proposed making another copy for filing. Mr. Takada said

Onegai-shimasu. Warui-kedo.
(Yes, please do that. Sorry to trouble you.)

Mr. Lerner realized that he had usually said *Hai* or *Hai, arigatoo* in a situation like this. He wondered if he should have said *Onegai-shimasu* instead.

*　　　*　　　*

When accepting an offer, it is most common to say

Onegai-shimasu.
お願いします。
(*lit.* I ask you to do so.)

This expression can be used in almost any situation, except when one has to be very polite or formal. In such cases you should say *Onegai-itashimasu.*

Sometimes foreigners say *Ii-desu* to mean "Fine" or "That sounds good." A student of ours once said *Sore-wa ii-desu* to an offer of a snack that she wanted but couldn't have. When someone has said

Nanika onomimono ikaga-desu-ka.
(Would you like something to drink?)

you can say *Hai, arigatoo-gozaimasu,* but it is better to add *onegai-shimasu* because the other person may wonder if you are politely declining with *Arigatoo-gozaimasu.* And saying just *Doozo* is not appropriate, either.

Between good friends or towards younger people *tanomu* is used instead of *Onegai-shimasu.* Between friends men will say *Tanomu-yo* and women *Tanomu-wa.*

It is good to add some expression of consideration as in

   Onegai-shimasu. Sumimasen-kedo.
   お願いします。 すみませんけど。

Warui-kedo is used in familiar conversation; to be polite, *Mooshiwake arimasen* or *Osoreirimasu* (I'm very sorry to trouble you) is used. Sometimes expressions such as the following are also added:

   Otesuu-desu-ga.
   (I'm sorry to trouble you.)
   Isogashii toki-ni sumimasen-kedo.
   (Sorry to trouble you when you're so busy.)
   Tasukarimasu.
   (That will be a great help to me.)

Avoiding long modifiers

Mr. Lerner received a telegram that one of his best friends had lost his father. He wanted to attend the funeral and asked Mr. Mori, the director of the company, for the day off. He said

Nagoya-ni sunde-iru tomodachi-no otoosan-no sooshiki-ni detai-node, ashita yasumasete-itadakemasu-ka.
(Could I be excused tomorrow because I want to attend the funeral of the father of a friend of mine living in Nagoya?)

*   *   *

To grammatically analyze Mr. Lerner's sentence above, the word *sooshiki* (funeral) is modified by a long phrase. In spoken language, using a long modifier should be avoided. Mr. Lerner could have said instead, for instance,

Jitsu-wa Nagoya-no tomodachi-ga otoosan-o nakushimashite . . .
実は　名古屋の　友だちが　お父さんを　なくしまして……
(A friend of mine in Nagoya lost his father.)

and the listener would have said *ee,* and he could have continued

Sore-de sooshiki-ga ashita-na-n-desu-ga, dekireba ikitai-to omoimasu-node, yasumasete-itadakenai-deshoo-ka.
(And the funeral will be held tomorrow. I would like to attend it, if possible, so could I be excused?)

In daily conversation, according to a survey by

the National Language Research Institute, fairly short sentences are used — very often composed of only two to three phrases. Longer sentences are used when explaining things, but still sentences of more than five or six phrases are rarely used. Saying something like

Kinoo Yoshida-san-to Shinjuku-de katta teepu-rekoodaa-ga kowareta-node, naoshite-morai-ni iku tokoro-desu.

(Since the tape recorder I bought in Shinjuku with Miss Yoshida yesterday broke, I'm going to have it fixed.)

would be too long. You should break it up as in

(1) *Kinoo Yoshida-san-to Shinjuku-de teepu-rekoodaa-o katta-n-desu-ga,* (2) *sore-ga kowareta-node* (3) *naoshite-morai-ni iku tokoro-desu.*

The first part does not have any long phrases. And between (1) and (2) there will certainly be *aizuchi* given by the listener; between (2) and (3), the listener will give *aizuchi* if you pause.

Introductory words with *ka*

Mr. Lerner wanted to find someone to teach him the basics of calligraphy, so he asked Miss Yoshida

Shodoo-no sensee, shirimasen-ka.

meaning "Do you know any teachers of calligraphy?" Miss Yoshida immediately called one of her friends and inquired; she said,

Dareka shodoo-o oshiete-kureru hito inai-deshoo-ka.
(I wonder if there is anyone teaching calligraphy.)

Mr. Lerner realized that his question somehow sounded abrupt when compared with Miss Yoshida's, and he wondered if one reason was that he did not use the word *dareka*.

*　　　*　　　*

Several question words are used with *ka* in this way, such as *dareka, dokoka, nanika, itsuka* and *doreka*. These words mean someone, some place, something, some time and some. They are used alone as in

Dareka imasen-ka. (Is anyone there?)
Nanika ochite-imasu. (Something has dropped.)

And they are also used before a noun which is modified by other words, as in

Nanika taberu mono arimasen-ka.

（Is there anything to eat?）
Dareka tetsudatte-kureru hito imasen-ka.
だれか　てつだってくれる　人　いませんか。
（Is there anyone who could help me?）

Dokoka koohii-no-oishii mise, shirimasen-ka.
（Do you know any place serving good coffee?）

Itsuka gotsugoo-no ii toki, goannai-shimasu.
いつか　ご都合の　いい　とき、ご案内します。
（I will take you some time when you are free.）

In these sentences, the first introductory words such as *nanika*, *dareka* and *dokoka* can be left out without changing the meaning. But although the meaning is not changed, the tone is different. Those without such introductory words sound abrupt. Through the use of such words as *dareka, dokoka, itsuka*, the listener can anticipate what kind of statement is going to follow. And this also helps the listener understand a long phrase made up of modifiers and a noun.

21

Ikimasu-ka vs. *ikimasen-ka*— use of the negative form in questions

Mr. Lerner wanted to invite some of his colleagues to his home, and when asking them to come, he thought he would use some other expression than *kite-kudasai*. He wondered if it is more polite to say

Kite-kudasaimasen-ka.

than

Kite-kudasaimasu-ka.

*   *   *

When asking questions, either the affirmative or negative form is used, with some difference between the two. Generally speaking, a negative question implies that the speaker wishes the response to be in the affirmative. In other words, when inviting someone, it shows more enthusiasm if one uses a negative question, as in

Issho-ni ikimasen-ka.
いっしょに　行きませんか。
Won't you go with me?)
Kore, meshiagatte-mite-kudasaimasen-ka.
(Won't you taste this?)
Chotto kore, mite-kurenai?
(Won't you take a look at this?)

On the other hand, to invite someone with reserve, one chooses the affirmative form. Saying

Issho-ni ikimasu-ka.
(Will you go with me?)
Kore, meshiagatte-mite-kudasaimasu-ka.
(Would you taste this?)

Chotto mite-kureru?
(Will you take a look at this?)

sounds more reserved.

Questions are also used when asking for permission. In this case, too, it sounds more reserved to use the affirmative. Saying

Kaette-mo ii-desu-ka.
帰っても　いいですか。
(May I go home?)
sounds more reserved than

Kaette-wa ikemasen-ka.
帰っては　いけませんか。
(Can't I go home?)

When a question is asked to obtain factual information also, the negative form implies that the speaker expects something to be true. While

Kore, sanman-en-desu-ka?
(Is this 30,000 yen?)
simply asks whether it is 30,000 yen or not,
Kore, sanman-en-ja arimasen-ka.
(Isn't this 30,000 yen?)

implies that the speaker expects it to be ¥30,000.

This is true for polite questions. When you want to identify someone politely, you can choose either of the following two, based on this difference in expectation.

Shitsuree-desu-ga, Katoo-sensee-de irasshaimasu-ka.
(Excuse me. Are you Professor Kato?)
Shitsuree-desu-ga, Katoo-sensee-dewa irasshaimasen-ka.
(Excuse me. Aren't you Professor Kato?)

. . .ta hoo-ga ii referring to someone else

Mr. Lerner and several of his colleagues were invited to Miss Yoshida's house last Saturday. At around nine o'clock Mr. Lerner thought he should be leaving, and said

Moo kaetta hoo-ga ii-desu.

meaning "I had better leave now." Then his colleagues looked at each other, and started getting ready to leave. Mr. Lerner wondered why they thought they should be leaving when he was referring to himself.

* * *

The expression *. . .ta hoo-ga ii* is usually used to refer to someone else. If you say

Neta hoo-ga ii-desu.

it usually refers to someone else and means "You/He/She/They had better go to bed." Therefore when Mr. Lerner said *kaetta hoo-ga ii*, his listeners thought that he meant "You had better leave now" or "All of us should leave now."

. . .ta hoo-ga ii is a general statement meaning "it is best to . . . ," and is not usually directed to the speaker himself. The speaker can use it by way of explaining the reason for his action as in

Hayaku itta hoo-ga ii-kara, moo demasu.
早く 行った ほうが いいから、もう 出ます。
(Since it is best to be there early, I am leaving now.)

but one does not say *moo deta hoo-ga ii-desu* to

24

refer to oneself.

It can also be used in speech to oneself with such particles as *na, kana* and *kashira* as in

> *Moo deta hoo-ga ii-na.*
> (I guess I had better leave now.)

One can use *. . .ta hoo-ga ii* in this way probably because one is treating oneself as someone else when talking to oneself.

Some appropriate expressions that Mr. Lerner could have used in a situation like the one mentioned above are;

> *Dewa, shitsuree-shimasu.*
> (Please excuse me now.)
> *Sorosoro shitsuree-shimasu.*
> (I should be leaving now.)

Using *ne* between phrases

Mr. Lerner happened to pass by Miss Yoshida when she was talking to someone, obviously her friend. She used *ne* fairly often between phrases as in

Sorede-ne, shikata-ga nai-kara-ne, itte-mitara-ne. . .
(So, there was no other way, and I went there, and. . .)

Mr. Lerner remembered that when she talked with her colleagues or superiors, she seldom used *ne* between phrases, but used it only at the end of a sentence as in

Kono-goro-wa samui hi-ga ooi-desu-ne.
(We are having many cold days now.)

*   *   *

The particle *ne* is used to ascertain whether the listener has understood or agreed, so it is more often used when the speaker is anxious to obtain the listener's reaction. In reserved conversation, *ne* is used only at the end of a sentence. In fact, insertion of this short word can change the tone of one's speech. If you say

Anoo, chotto onegai-ga aru-n-desu-ga.
あのう……
(Excuse me. Would you do me a favor?)

it sounds reserved. But if you add *ne* after *anoo* as in

Ano-ne, chotto onegai-ga aru-n-desu-ga.
あのね……

it suddenly sounds much more familiar.

Between good friends and family members, one sometimes uses *ne* after each phrase as in

Ano-ne, chotto-ne, onegai-ga-ne, aru-n-da-kedo-ne.
(Say, will you do me a little favor?)

Using *ne* frequently between phrases makes the tone very familiar, so it is done only in familiar conversation.

To avoid sounding too familiar, one sometimes uses *desu-ne* instead of *ne* as in

Jitsu-wa-desu-ne, chotto onegai-ga arimashite.
じつはですね、ちょっと　お願いが　ありまして。
(As a matter of fact, I'd like to ask you to do a little favor for me.)

But this *desu-ne* is not used as often as just *ne* in familiar conversation. In fact, the frequency of *ne* is proportionate to familiarity; when one is very reserved, or when talking impersonally like on a radio program, *ne* is seldom used even at the end of the sentence, to say nothing of between phrases.

The negative form of . . . *soo-desu*

Yesterday evening when Miss Yoshida was getting ready to leave the office and looked out the window, she noticed that it looked like it was going to rain, and said

> *Ame-ni narisoo-desu-ne.*
> (It looks like it is going to rain.)

And she asked Mr. Takada if he was also leaving, but he answered

> *Mada kaeresoo-mo nai-kara, osaki-ni doozo.*
> (It doesn't seem that I will be able to leave very soon, so please go ahead.)

Mr. Lerner had learned the expression . . . *soo-desu* (it looks like . . .) as in *ame-ga furisoo-desu/da,* but he did not know that the negative form of this expression is not . . . *soo-ja arimasen/nai* but . . . *soo-mo arimasen* or . . . *soo-mo nai.*

*   *   *

When describing things, . . . *soo* is added to the stem of verbs and adjectives as in these two examples:

1. *Yamada-san-wa nandaka ureshisoo-desu-ne.*
   (Miss Yamada somehow looks happy today.)
2. *Kono ame-wa yamisoo-desu.*
   (It looks like it is going to clear up.)

To change these into the negative, two different forms are used depending on the meaning of the sentence. When the words with . . . *soo* are used to describe the appearance of someone or something as in (1) above, . . . *soo-ja arimasen/nai* is used as in

    Yamada-san-wa amari ureshisoo-ja nakatta-ne.
    山田さんは　あまり　うれしそうじゃ　なかつたね。
    (Miss Yamada didn't look very happy.)

Usually adjectives are used in this way; . . . *ku nasasoo* is also used as the negative form.

    Yamada-san-wa amari ureshiku nasasoo-datta-ne.

On the other hand, when changing . . . *soo* expressions which describe change or possibility as in (2) above and Mr. Takada's answer, . . . *soo-mo arimasen/nai* is used instead as in

    Kono ame-wa sugu-niwa yamisoo-mo arimasen.
    この　雨は　すぐには　やみそうも　ありません。
    (It doesn't look like the rain will be clearing up very soon.)
    Ashita-made-niwa dekisoo-mo nai.
    (It doesn't look like I will be able to finish it by tomorrow.)

Sometimes . . . *soo-nimo arimasen/nai* is also used. Expressions with . . . *soo* added to most verbs are changed into the negative in this way.

Responding to compliments

The other day Mr. Lerner and Miss Yoshida visited Mr. Okada, a mutual acquaintance. When they were shown into the guest room, Miss Yoshida complimented him on his house. He first flatly denied this saying *Iie,* but when Miss Yoshida said that it was very nice and quiet, he said

Shizukana koto-wa shizuka-desu-ga, chotto fuben-de . . .
しずかな　ことは　しずかですが、ちょっと
不便で……
(It is quiet all right, but it's not very convenient.)

* * *

How to respond to a compliment differs depending on one's relationship with the other person. Between good friends or family members, one can easily accept a compliment, as in

A: *Ii sebiro-dane.* (That's a nice suit.)
B: *Un, maa-ne. Takakatta-n-dayo.*
(Well, it's not bad, is it? It cost me a lot.)
A: *Yoku niau-yo.* (It looks good on you.)
B: *Arigatoo.* (Thanks.)

With someone you have to show modesty and reserve toward, however, you should not accept a compliment unconditionally. In polite conversation, therefore, one usually denies a compliment at first and when necessary, admits some good point and adds some weak point.

To take one example, the most common phrase for praising a house is

30

Ii osumai-desu-ne.
いい　おすまいですね。
(You have a very nice house.)

Usually the host or hostess simply says *Iie,* and dismisses the matter quickly, saying something like "Please make yourself comfortable." And when the visitor still continues with his compliments and says something like it's nice and quiet or conveniently located, and if this is true, the host or hostess will conditionally admit it, very often using the . . . *koto-wa . . . desu-ga* expression as in

Ee, eki-kara chikai koto-wa chikai-desu-ga . . .
(Yes, it's close to the station all right, but . . .)

Or, when the visitor has mentioned the garden, the host or hostess will say something like

Ee, niwa-mo aru koto-wa arimasu-ga . . .
(Yes, we have a garden all right, but . . .)

And after such remarks, the host or hostess will add some weak point as in

Eki-kara chikai koto-wa chikai-desu-ga, chotto mawari-ga urusakute . . .
(. . . , but the neighborhood is not quiet.)
Niwa-mo aru koto-wa arimasu-ga, hiatari-ga amari yoku nai-node . . .
(. . . , but it does not get much sunshine.)

. . . te-shimau used to show regret

Yesterday afternoon when Mr. Lerner was talking with Mr. Mori, the director of the company, in his office, Miss Yoshida came in holding a broken vase and said

Kono kabin, otoshite-shimaimashite, mooshiwake arimasen.
(I'm very sorry to have dropped this vase.)

Mr. Mori told her not to worry, but Mr. Lerner wondered if she had used the *. . . te-shimau* expression to add politeness to the apology or if it is always added to apologetic expressions.

*　　*　　*

The *. . . te-shimau* expression is used to show either the completion of an action of a feeling of regret. The first use is seen in such sentences:

Moo kaite-shimatta-kara, hitoiki ireyoo.
(Since I have finished writing it, I will take a break.)
Yonde-shimattara moto-no tokoro-e kaeshite-kudasai.
読んでしまったら　もとの　ところへ　返してくだ
さい。
(When you have finished reading it, please return it to where it was.)

Miss Yoshida used this expression in the second usage, namely of indicating regret. One often uses this expression in this way in daily life, as in

Kanojo-ga yamete-shimatta-node, shokuba-ga sabishiku narimashita-ne.

(Since she left the office, we often miss her.)

Kyoo-wa ukkari-shite-ite, densha-o norisugoshite-shimatta.

(I was absent-minded today and rode the train past my station.)

When offering an apology, . . . te-shimau is often used to emphasize the speaker's regret, as in

Okaeshi-suru-no-ga osoku natte-shimatte, sumimasen.

お返しするのが　おそく　なってしまって、すみません。

(I'm sorry I didn't return it to you sooner — *lit.* I became late in returning it.)

Shitsureena koto-o mooshiagete-shimaimashite, mooshiwake gozaimasen.

(I'm awfully sorry I made an impolite remark.)

Since . . . te-shimau tends to imply regret, one should not use it about happy events. If you said *Yamamoto-san-wa kekkon-shite-shimaimashita,* (Miss Yamamoto ended up getting married), the listener might suspect that you have some reason to be disappointed at her marriage.

Common contractions

When Mr. Lerner passed by where Miss Yoshida was talking with a young colleague at lunchtime, he heard her saying

Ima yonderu. Yonjattara motte-kitageru.
いま　読んでる。読んじゃったら　持ってきたげる。

He understood that she meant that she was reading the book in question and that she would bring it to her colleague when she had finished reading it, but he was surprised at the familiar tone and use of contractions.

*　　　*　　　*

Several kinds of contracted forms are used in familiar conversation. Miss Yoshida contracted *yonde-iru* into *yonderu, yonde-shimattara* into *yonjattara,* and *motte-kite-ageru* into *motte-kitageru.* The following is an explanation of some common contractions, including those used by Miss Yoshida.

1. The *i* sound in *iru, iku* and *irassharu* is very often dropped:

Omachi-shite-masu. (I'll be waiting for you.) from *Omachi-shite-imasu.*

Itte-rasshai. (Goodbye, said to a family member going out) from *Itte-irasshai.*

This dropping of the *i* sound is seen in fairly polite speech, too.

2. Expressions composed of the *te* form followed by another verb or by *wa* are contracted as follows:

kaichatta	(I have written it)	from *kaite-shimatta*
yonjatta	(I have read it)	from *yonde-shimatta*

kaitoita	(I wrote it beforehand)	from *kaite-oita*
yondoita	(I read it beforehand)	from *yonde-oita*
kaitageru	(I'll write it for you)	from *kaite-ageru*
yondageru	(I'll read it for you)	from *yonde-ageru*
kaicha ikemasen	(You shouldn't write it)	from *kaite-wa ikemasen*
yonja ikemasen	(You shouldn't read it)	from *yonde-wa ikemasen*

3. . . . *kereba* in such phrases as *yokereba* (if it is good) and *ikanakereba* (if I don't go) are contracted into either *kya* or *kerya*.

yasukya	(if it's inexpensive)	from *yasukereba*
yasukerya	(if it's inexpensive)	from *yasukereba*
kakanakya naranai	(I have to write it)	from *kakanakereba naranai*
kakanakerya naranai	(I have to write it)	from *kakanakereba naranai*

4. In addition to these common contractions, sometimes the *ra* and *re* sounds become *n*.

wakannai	(I don't understand)	from *wakaranai*
kawannai	(It doesn't change)	from *kawaranai*
mirannai	(I can't see it)	from *mirarenai*

Connecting two sentences (1)
Sore-wa

On Monday morning Mr. Lerner wanted to tell
Miss Yoshida about his weekend and said

Kinoo Shinjuku-de eega-o mimashita.
(I saw a movie in Shinjuku yesterday.)
He started to say that the movie was very good, and
wondered if he should say *Sore-wa ii eega-deshita* or
Sono eega-wa ii eega-deshita or simply *Ii eega-
deshita.*

*　　　*　　　*

When the speaker has started talking about a
certain subject, and is going to continue, the subject is usually left out in the second sentence. For
instance, if you want to say that your house is
located in Nakano, is close to the station, and is
convenient, you should say

*Uchi-wa Nakano-desu. Eki-kara chikakute benri-
desu.*
うちは　中野です。駅から　近くて　便利です。

One does not usually repeat *Uchi-wa* or *Sore-wa* in
the second sentence. It would sound strange to say
Uchi-wa eki-kara chikakute . . . or *Sore-wa eki-kara
chikakute . . .* in the second sentence.

In the same way, the object of a verb in the first
sentence is not usually repeated in the second
sentence, either. For instance, it is appropriate to
say

*Ano mise-de sakki ohiru-o tabemashita.
Oishikatta-desu.*

(I had lunch at that restaurant a while ago. It was good.)

One does not say *Ano mise-de sakki ohiru-o tabemashita. Sore-wa/Sono ohiru-wa oishikatta-desu* unless one wants to call special attention to the meal.

Thus, in Mr. lerner's case, if he wanted to dimiss the matter quickly, he should have said *Ii eega-deshita*. If, on the other hand, he wanted to talk about the movie in detail, he could have said something like

> *Sono eega-wa Kurosawa-no eega-de, daibu mae-no-desu-ga . . .*
> (That was a Kurosawa movie of many years ago, and . . .)

This means that if you repeated *Sore-wa* or *Sono eega-wa,* the listener would expect you to describe it fully or give your impressions fully. If you just dismissed the matter and immediately went on to another subject, the listener would have to adjust to the unexpected development in the conversation. Avoiding the use of an unnecessary subject in the second sentence will help your Japanese sound more fluent and make it easier for a Japanese listener to listen to.

... *te kureru* used to express the speaker's happiness

When Mr. Lerner was getting ready to leave the office yesterday evening, Miss Yoshida looked out the window and said

Aa, yokatta. Ame-ga yande-kureta.
ああ、よかった。雨が　やんでくれた。
(Oh, good. It's stopped raining.)

Mr. Lerner was interested in this expression. Although the rain obviously had no intention of being kind to Miss Yoshida, she used the expression ... *te-kureru* as if the rain had done her a special favor.

* * *

The expression ... *te-kureru* is usually used to indicate someone's doing a favor for the speaker, as in

Yoshida-san-ga kite-kuremashita.
(Miss Yoshida kindly came to see me.)

To be humble, ... *te-kudasaru* is used as in

Sensee-ga oide-kudasaimashita.
(The professor kindly came to see me.)

This expression shows the speaker's gratitude for someone's kind action, and if the speaker is not greateful for the action, the action can be described without using ... *te-kureru* or ... *te-kudasaru* as in

Yoshida-san-ga kimashita.
Sensee-ga oide-ni narimashita.

Conversely, if the speaker is grateful for someone's action, he uses . . . *te-kureru* even if the performer of the action does not mean to be kind. For instance, a teacher will sometimes say

Ano gakusee-wa yoku benkyoo-shite-kureru.
(That student studies hard.)

when he is happy about his student's hard work. Or, rather, we should say that he is grateful to his student for making him happy. Also, one will often say

Hanaseba wakatte-kureru-deshoo.
(He will understand if I explain.)

when the speaker wishes someone to understand.

This usage of . . . *te-kureru* is sometimes extended toward impersonal phenomena, as in Miss Yoshida's statement above. The speaker will express his happiness about a desired change in the weather as in

Yatto yuki-ga futte-kureta.
(Finally it snowed.)

to describe an ardent skier's happiness. This expression is also used to convey the speaker's disappointment or irritation as in

Nakanaka yuki-ga futte-kurenai.
(The snow is taking its time coming.)

Hayaku haru-ni natte-kurenai-kana.
早く 春に なってくれないかな。
(I wish spring would come soon.)

Praising one's family

The other day Mr. Lerner met a friend of his at a party and introduced him to Miss Yoshida. This friend has a Japanese wife, and when Miss Yoshida asked him whether he speaks Japanese with her, he said no, and added

Kanai-wa eego-ga taihen joozu-desu-kara.
(My wife speaks English very well.)

Later Mr. Lerner asked Miss Yoshida if his praise had seemed strange to her. She answered that it was all right because he was a foreigner.

* * *

Praising or accepting a compliment concerning a family member in public is similar to accepting a compliment to oneself. Between good friends one can freely praise or accept a compliment to one's family, but when talking politely in social situations, one usually refrains from doing so.

It is most reserved to simply say

Kanai-ga eego-o hanashimasu-node.
家内が　英語を　話しますので。
(Because my wife speaks English.)

and to go on to another subject without bothering to praise her English. This is also true when one responds to a compliment about other family members.

If you want to refer to your wife's being better at English than you are at Japanese, you might say something like

Kanai-no eego-no hoo-ga mashi-desu-kara.

(My wife's English is not as bad as my Japanese.)
or

Kanai-no eego-mo taishita koto-wa arimasen-ga, watashi-no nihongo-yori mashi-desu-node.

(My wife is not very good at English, but her English is not as bad as my Japanese.)

And if you want to praise her English in a reserved way, you might use a preliminary remark like

Watashi-ga yuu-nowa hen-desu-ga, kanai-wa wariai eego-ga dekimasu-node.

(*lit.* It may sound strange for me to say so, but my wife speaks English fairly well.)

The remark made by Miss Yoshida that it was all right because the speaker was a foreigner reflects the thinking of many Japanese. Accepting praise freely or praising one's own family will not sound impolite, nor will it offend Japanese listeners. In fact, some Japanese may wish they could do the same thing. But a foreigner doing this should be aware that he is being accepted as a foreigner, and if he wants to really talk like a Japanese, he will be wise to conform to the Japanese custom in this matter.

Nandemo used when conveying uncertain information

Mr. Lerner noticed that Mr. Kobayashi, a young colleague of his, had been absent for several days, and asked Miss Yoshida about it. She answered

Nandemo okaasan-ga byooki-da-soo-desu-kedo.
(I heard that his mother is sick or something.)

and turned to Mr. Takada for confirmation; he said

Ee, nandemo sonna hanashi-deshita-yo.
ええ、なんでも そんな 話でしたよ。
(Yes, I heard that kind of story.)

Mr. Lerner wondered what this *nandemo* stands for.

* * *

Nandemo is used, as one usage, to mean "anything" as in

A: *Nani-ga ii-desu-ka.* (What would you like to have?)

B: *Nandemo ii-desu.* (Anything will do.)

But as Miss Yoshida and Mr. Takada used it, *nandemo* indicates that the speaker is going to give some uncertain information. If Miss Yoshida had said

Okaasan-ga byooki-da-soo-desu.
(I heard that his mother is sick.)

without using *nandemo,* it would have implied that she was certain about the information.

In this usage, the last part of the sentence usually ends with such phrases as:

. . . *soo-desu.* (I heard/understand that . . .)

. . . to yuu hanashi-desu. (I heard that . . .)
. . . to yuu koto-desu. (I heard that . .)

Nandemo is used in this way to imply that the speaker does not want to commit himself to the information. Sometimes the speaker chooses this phrase when conveying a bit of information that is unpleasant, whether or not he believes in the truth of the information, as in

Nandemo daibu shakkin-ga aru-soo-desu-yo.
なんでも　だいぶ　借金が　あるそうですよ。
(I heard that he has a lot of debts or something.)

Ano futari, nandemo tootoo wakareru koto-ni shita-tte hanashi-desu.
(I heard that they finally decided to get a divorce.)

... *te-wa* used to emphasize contrast between two phrases

When Mr. Takada was leaving the office yesterday evening, he said that he was going drinking with some of his colleagues. Miss Yoshida admonished him saying that it was not good for the health to drink every day. Mr. Takada smiled and said

Wakatcha iru-kedo-ne.
わかっちゃ　いるけどね。
(I know but . . .)

Mr. Lerner understood what he meant but wondered if *wakatcha iru* is more emphatic than *wakatte-iru.*

* * *

The form *wakatcha* is the contraction of *wakatte-wa; wakatcha iru* is the same as *wakatte-wa iru.* The *wa* added to *wakatte* emphasizes the contrast between two phrases. For example, *wa* is added as in

Shigoto-wa suki-da-ga, asobu-nowa kirai-da.
(I like to work, but I don't like having fun.)

Mr. Takada did not complete his sentence, but the whole sentence would have been something like

Wakatte-wa iru-kedo, yamerarenai-n-desu-yo.
(I know that, but I can't stop it.)

In fact, there is a common expression *Wakatcha iru-kedo yamerarenai,* and *yamerarenai* is usually understood without being mentioned.

The meaning would have been clear if Mr.

44

Takada had not added *wa* to *wakatte,* but adding *wa* makes the contrast between *wakatte-iru* and *yamerarenai* even clearer.

The *wa* with this function is added to several other *te* phrases as in

> *Tanonde-wa miru-keredo (dame-kamo shirenai).*
> たのんでは みるけれど。
> (I will surely ask him, but he may say no.)
> *Katte-wa aru-keredo (doko-ni oita-ka wasureta).*
> (I certainly bought it, but I don't remember where I placed it.)
> *Kashite-wa ageru-keredo (sugu kaeshite-yo).*
> (I will lend it to you, but I want you to return it very soon.)

45

Expressions used to ask
for a special favor

Mr. Lerner went to Miss Yoshida to ask her to type something, but Mr. Takada was talking with her, apparently asking her to do some work of his in a hurry. Miss Yoshida did not say yes right away, and Mr. Takada then said

Onegai-da-kara.
お願いだから。
(Please! — *lit.* Because I am beseeching you.)

Miss Yoshida laughed and gave in. Later Mr. Lerner asked Mr. Takada why Miss Yoshida had laughed; he explained that the phrase he used sounded like women's speech, and it had amused her.

* * *

Onegai-da-kara is used in familiar conversation, mainly by children or women, when asking for a special favor from their superiors or those in a stronger position. Children will often use it when asking their parents to buy something or give them special permission to do something, but parents, especially fathers, will not use it toward their children. When Mr. Takada used it with Miss Yoshida, he sounded like a boy asking his mother to do him a special favor; it sounded funny and out of place, and therefore it succeeded in persuading her to do his work.

Without being humorous, Mr. Takada could have said

Tanomu-kara.
たのむから。
(Please. — *lit.* Because I am asking you.)

46

for the same purpose. This expression is used mostly by men toward equals and inferiors.

In polite conversation one uses such expressions as

Nantoka onegai-shimasu.
なんとか　お願いします。
(Would you please do it? — *lit.* I ask you to manage it somehow.)
Nantoka onegai-dekinai-deshoo-ka.
(Would you please do it for me? — *lit.* I wonder if you could manage it somehow.)

Sometimes *Soko-o* (that respect) precedes the above expressions as in

Soko-o nantoka onegai-dekinai-deshoo-ka.

To show reserve, the following phrases are often said first

Murina onegai-da-towa omoimasu-ga,
(I know I am asking you to do something very hard, but)
Muri-o mooshiagete sumimasen-ga,
(I am sorry to ask you to do something very hard, but)

And very often the last phrase is left out, as in

Murina onegai-da-towa omoimasu-ga, soko-o nantoka . . .

Hayaku-kara taihen-desu-ne
—leaving out a verb phrase

Mr. Lerner left home an hour earlier than usual yesterday because he wanted to finish some urgent work at the office. Mrs. Yamada, his neighbor, was cleaning the street in front of her house and said

Maa, hayaku-kara taihen-desu-ne.
(It's hard on you to have to be up and leaving so early.)

Mr. Lerner was interested in this expression; after *hayaku-kara,* the verb phrase for "to go to work" had been left out. He wondered if there are other cases when the verb phrase is left out in this way.

*　　　*　　　*

The expression *Taihen-desu-ne* (That's tough) is often preceded by phrases that describe the situation; in such cases the verb phrase is usually left out.

Osoku-made (　　　　) taihen-desu-ne.
おそくまで　たいへんですね。
(It's tough that you have to work until late.)
Mainichi (　　　) taihen-desu-ne.
毎日　たいへんですね。
(It's tough that you have to study hard every day.)
Samui-noni (　　　) taihen-desu-ne.
(It's tough that you have to go out to work when it is so cold.)
Ohitori-de (　　　) taihen-desu-ne.
(It's tough that you must take care of your children all by yourself.)

48

In these sentences, phrases such as *hataraku-nowa* (to work), *benkyoo-suru-nowa* (to study) and *kodomo-no sewa-o suru-nowa* (to take care of children) are understood and left out.

Verb phrases are often left out in this way in expressions of gratitude and apology, too, when it is obvious what action is referred to.

Konna-ni osoku (ojama-shite/denwa-shite) sumimasen.

こんなに　おそく　すみません。

(I'm sorry for visiting/calling this late.)

Konna-ni takusan (itadaite/motte-kite-itadaite) sumimasen.

(Thank you for giving/bringing me so much.)

Wazawaza (shirasete-kurete) arigatoo.

(Thank you for taking the trouble to inform me.)

Kurasu, ikiru and sumu
(to live)

Mr. Lerner and his colleagues were talking about their experiences with pets during their lunch hour yesterday. Mr. Lerner talked about the cat they once had that lived to be quite old; he said

Uchi-no neko-wa juugo-sai-made kurashimashita.

meaning "Our cat lived until she was 15 years old." They understood, but Miss Yoshida later told him that he should have said

. . . made ikimashita.
or
. . . made nagaiki-shimashita.

Mr. Lerner remembered that he had studied the three verbs, *ikiru, kurasu* and *sumu,* but now he was not sure about the difference between them.

* * *

The word *kurasu* refers to human life; it actually means "to live a human life." It is used as in

Machi-no hito-ga shinsetsu-na-node, kurashi-yasui.
(The townspeople are so kind that my life is easy.)
Bukka-ga takakute, kurashi-nikui.
物価が　高くて、暮らしにくい。
(Prices are so high that our life is not easy.)

Kurasu cannot be used with living things other than human beings unless they are being personified. If you said something like

Daitoshi-niwa gokiburi-ga takusan kurashite-imasu.

(There are many cockroaches living in big cities.)

it would make one imagine cockroaches earning a livelihood and supporting their families.

On the other hand, *ikiru* refers to biological life; namely, it concerns whether creatures are alive or dead. For instance, we often say something like

Ikite-iru uchi-ni ningen-ga tsuki-e ikeru yoo-ni naru-kana.

生きている　うちに　人間が　月へ　行ける　よう
に　なるかな。

(I wonder if I will live long enough to see human beings start traveling to the moon.)

When a human being or an animal lives to be very old, *naga-iki* (*lit.* long-living) is used to describe it.

Sumu refers to residing in a certain place, as in
三年前から　東京に　住んでいます。
Sannen-mae-kara Tookyoo-ni sunde-imasu.

(I have lived in Tokyo for three years.)
Kono kuni-niwa tora-wa sunde-inai.
(There are no tigers living in this country).

Ichido (once) used when making a suggestion

Mr. Okada came for a business discussion with Mr. Lerner and Mr. Takada yesterday afternoon. After the discussion, he complained about his heart; he said that he had seen several doctors but had not yet been able to find the right cure. Then Mr. Takada mentioned the name of a doctor he knew well, and said

Ichido mite-morattara doo-desu-ka.
一度　みてもらったら　どうですか。
(Why don't you consult him? — *lit.* How will it be if you have him look at you once?)

It was just a common expression, but Mr. Lerner realized that he himself had not used the word *ichido* (once) in such cases and wondered if it was really necessary.

*　　　*　　　*

Ichido by itself means "once"; *-do* means "time" or "times" as in

Kobayashi-san-niwa ichido aimashita.
(I met Mr. Kobayashi once.)
Asoko-wa nido-bakari ikimahita.
(I went there two times.)

When *ichido* is used for making a suggestion, it adds the meaning of "just try and see." Mr. Takada could have said to Mr. Takada

Mite-morattara doo-desu-ka.

instead, without adding *ichido,* in the case above. But by adding *ichido,* he implied that he was only suggesting it and not insisting on it, and because of this his suggestion did not sound pressing or demanding. In the same way one will say, while recommending some medicine,

Ichido nonde-goran-nasai-yo. Yoku kiku-kara.
(Take this; it will surely be effective.)
Damasareta-to omotte ichido nonde-mite-kudasai.
(Take it and see. I guarantee that it is good. —. *lit.* Think that you have been cheated by me and take it and see.)

Several other expressions meaning "one . . ." are often used when making suggestions. For instance, *hitotsu* (one piece), *ippai* (one glass), *hito-kuchi* (one bite, one mouthful) and *hito-yasumi* (one rest) are used as in

Hitotsu doozo.
ひとつ どうぞ。
(Please have some — offering food)
Ippai ikaga-desu-ka.
(Would you like some? — offering a drink)
Hito-kuchi tabete-mite-kudasai.
(Please try some — offering food)
Kokora-de hito-yasumi shimasen-ka.
(How about resting a while?)

53

Expressions indicating change

Mr. Lerner and Mr. Takada had lunch together at a fastfood place while they were out on business. They noticed that there were several women, apparently housewives, having lunch with their young children there. Mr. Takada remarked

Kono-goro-wa okusan-tachi-mo daibu gaishoku-suru yoo-ni natta-n-desu-ne.
(Recently housewives have come to eat out a lot.)

Mr. Lerner agreed, and at the same time wondered whether *yoo-ni naru* must always be added to a verb to indicate change.

* * *

To indicate change, the most basic expression is to add *naru* to nouns, adjectives and verbs.

1. with nouns (. . . *ni naru*)
    Moo sugu haru-ni narimasu-ne.
    (It will soon be spring.)
    Daigaku-o sotsugyoo-shitara sarariiman-ni naru tsumori-desu.
    (I plan to become a businessman when I graduate from college.)
2. with adjectives (. . . *ku naru/. . .ni naru*)
    Kore-kara dandan atatakaku narimasu.
    (It will become gradually warmer from now on.)
    Yuugata-ni naru-to nigiyaka-ni narimasu.
    (It becomes lively in the evening.)
3. with verbs (. . . *yoo-ni naru*)
    Kodomo-ga uchi-no shigoto-o tetsudau yoo-ni natta.

(Our children have come to help with the housework.)

Seeji ni kanshin-o motsu yoo-ni natta.

(They have come to be more concerned with politics.)

But with verbs which indicate change, *yoo-ni naru* is not added.

Ano-hito saikin kawarimashita-ne.
(He has changed recently, hasn't he?)
Kono-goro sukoshi yasemashita/futorimashita.
(I have recently lost/gained a little weight.)

... *te-kuru* and ... *te-iku* are added to *naru* and other verbs that indicate change; the former indicates change that has been going on up to the present and the latter indicates change that will keep going on from the present.

Daibu atatakaku natte-kimashita.
だいぶ　あたたかく　なってきました。
(It has become fairly warm.)
Bukka-wa dandan agatte-iku-deshoo.
物価は　だんだん　あがっていくでしょう。
(Prices will keep going up.)

. . . (nai)-ka-to omoimashite . . .
used for polite requests

Mr. Okada came for some business discussions with Mr. Lerner and Mr. Takada the other day. When the discussions for the day were finished, he said, while taking out another set of papers,

Kochira-no hoo-mo kangaete-itadakenai-ka-to omoimashite . . .
(I wondered if you could consider this too — *lit.* I thought if you could not consider this too, and . . .)

Mr. Lerner had noticed that the Japanese often use *. . . (nai)-ka-to omoimashite* when making a polite request and he wondered if the last part of the sentence could be *omoimashita* (I thought) instead of *omoimashite* (I thought and . . .).

*　　　*　　　*

When Mr. Okada said *. . . kangaete-itadakenai-ka-to omoimashite,* he left out the ending of the sentence, which would have been something like

. . . motte-kimashita. (I brought it.)

In this way the Japanese often leave out such phrases as

. . . onegai-ni kimashita. (I came to ask this favor.)
. . . mairimashita. (I came — humble.)

after *. . . (nai)-ka-to omoimashite* to show reserve. For example,

Chotto tetsudatte-itadakenai-ka-to omoimashite . . .

56

ちょっと　てつだっていただけないかと　思いまし
て……

(I came to ask if you could help me.)

Chotto tetsudatte-moraenai-ka-to omotte . . .

ちょっと　てつだってもらえないかと　思って……

(I came to ask if you can help me — less polite.)

In this expression one should use the *te* form,
. . . to omoimashite or *. . . to omotte,* rather than *. . .
to omoimashita* or *. . . to omotta.* If you simply said

Kangaete-itadakenai-ka-to omoimashita.

instead of *. . . to omoimashite,* without implying
that you came to ask a favor, it would sound as if
you had once thought of asking but then had given
up the idea.

As the *. . . to omoimashite* phrase itself
describes the speaker's idea, the expression *. . .
(nai)-ka-to omoimashite* is used not only for making
a request but also for making a proposal or suggestion, as in

*Kore-ga ichiban oniai-ja nai-ka-to omoimashite
. . .*

(I thought this might suit you best — so I
bought it for you.)

Nanika-no oyaku-ni tatsu-ka-to omoimashite . . .

(I thought it might be of some use to you — so I
brought it to you.)

Expressions for reporting something

When Mr. Lerner arrived at the office yesterday morning, Miss Yoshida gave him a message from Mr. Okada, who was scheduled to meet with Mr. Lerner and Mr. Mori, saying

Jippun-hodo okureru soo-desu.
(I heard that he would be about 10 minutes late.)

Then she called Mr. Mori on the intercom and said

Okada-san-kara denwa-ga arimashite, mooshi-wake nai-ga jippun-hodo okureru-to yuu koto-deshita.
(Mr. Okada called and said that he was sorry but he would be about 10 minutes late.)

Mr. Lerner noticed that she had used two completely different expressions to convey the same message.

* * *

There are several expressions used for conveying a message.

1. *. . . soo-desu*
The simplest form is to use *. . . soo-desu* as in Miss Yoshida's report to Mr. Lerner.

Yamada-san-wa kaisha-o yameta soo-desu.
山田さんは　会社を　やめた　そうです。
(I heard that Mr. Yamada has quit his company.)
Terebi-no tenki-yohoo-da-to, konban ame-ni naru soo-desu.

(The TV weather forecast said that it will rain this evening.)

2.　... to yuu koto-desu

　... *to yuu koto-desu* is used when conveying a message in a formal way. Miss Yoshida used this when talking to the director of the company. Newscasters on TV or radio also use it, as in

　Shushoo-no kaeri-wa asu-no yuugata-ni naru-to yuu koto-desu.
　首相の　帰りは　あすの　夕方に　なると　いう
ことです。
　(It is reported that the prime minister will return tomorrow evening.)

3.　... tte

　In informal conversation ... *tte* is used; it means "I heard that . . ." or ". . . said that . . ."

　Okada-san jippun-gurai okureru-tte.
　岡田さん　十分ぐらい　おくれるって。
　(Mr. Okada said that he would be about 10 minutes late.)
　Ima warui kaze-ga hayatte-ru-n-da-tte.
　(I heard that a bad type of flu is spreading now.)

Mitsukeru and *mitsukaru*

Yesterday afternoon, Mr. Lerner was looking for a paper he had misplaced a few days before. Miss Yoshida was helping him. After a while he found it and said

A, *mitsukemashita*. (I've found it.)

Then she said

Mitsukatte yokatta-desu-ne.
(I'm glad you've found it.)

Mr. Lerner wondered if it was all right to say *Mitsukete yokatta-desu-ne* instead, because both *mitsukeru* and *mitsukaru* are used to refer to finding something, and the difference is that one is a transitive verb and the other intransitive.

*   *   *

Verbs which are usually preceded by a direct object plus the particle *o* are said to be transitive and verbs which never so occur are said to be intransitive. There are several sets of transitive and intransitive verbs.

Some of the more important ones are:

1.	*-eru, -aru*	*mitsukeru* (to find) *kakeru* (to hang, etc.) *kaeru* (to change)	*mitsukaru* (be found) *kakaru* (be hung, etc.) *kawaru* (be changed)
2.	*-eru, -u*	*tsukeru* (to attach)	*tsuku* (be attached)

3.	-osu, -oru	naosu (to cure)	naoru (be cured)
4.	-osu, -iru	okosu (to wake up)	okiru (be awakened, get up)
5.	-asu, -eru	samasu (to cool)	sameru (be cooled)
6.	-esu, -ieru	kesu (to extinguish)	kieru (be extinguish- ed)

Thus, it is grammatically correct to say

Shorui-o mitsukemashita. (I found the paper.)
Shorui-ga mitsukarimashita. (The paper was found.)

But in actual usage, when one has found something that one has been looking for, it is common to say

Mitsukatta. 見つかった。
(It has been found.)

or

Atta. (Here it is — *lit*. It was here.)

Mitsukemashita or *Mitsuketa* is used when finding something that has been intentionally hidden. Thus, when finding someone doing something he does not want you to know about, you will say

A, mitsuketa. あ、見つけた。
(I caught you.)

It sounds strange to say *Mitsukemashita* when finding something that you yourself have misplaced. It also sounds awkward to say *Mitsukete yokatta-desu-ne* in such a case.

Connecting two sentences (2)
De, . . .

Mr. Lerner recently noticed that many Japanese use *de* for connecting sentences. Just yesterday afternoon, he counted the number of times *de* was used while listening to Mr. Kato, one of his colleagues, talk at a meeting, and was surprised at the frequency of its use. Mr. Kato talked like this:

Mazu, sengetsu dai-ichian-ga dekimashita. De, hiyoo-no keesan-o shimashita tokoro, chotto suuji-ga ookiku narimashita. De, . . .
(We made the first plan last month, and then calculated the cost and found that it would be too much. So, . . .)

*   *   *

De is used to connect two sentences; it corresponds to such English expressions as "and," "and so," "and then" and "that is why." For example,

Atarashii keekaku-ga dekimashita. De, minasan-no okangae-o ukagaitai-n-desu-ga.
新しい 計画が できました。で、みなさんの お考えを うかがいたいんですが。
(A new plan has been made, and I'd like your opinions about it.)

Yamada-san-ga kyuubyoo-de nyuuin-shimashita. De, kawari-ni Kawakami-san-ni tanomu koto-ni narimashita.
(Mr. Yamada suddenly fell ill and was hospitalized. So, it was decided that we ask Mr. Kawakami to take over his work.)

Hantai-ga igai-ni ookatta. De, shibaraku miokuru koto-ni shita wake-da.

(Surprisingly many were opposed. That's why I decided to postpone it for the time being.)

Sometimes *de* is used simply to continue talking. In such cases, *de* can be left out without changing the meaning.

And *de* is also used to encourage the speaker to continue, as in

A: *Kinoo ano-hito-ni guuzen aimashite-ne.*
B: *Soo-desu-ka. De?*
　　そうですか。で？
A: *De, ano hanashi, tsutaete-okimashita.*

(A: I happened to meet him yesterday.
B: Did you? And?
A: So, I told him about that matter.)

De is similar to *sore-de* and *soko-de*; the difference is that *de* is more familiar than the other two.

Pikapika and *pikari* — mimetic words

Mr. Lerner and Miss Yoshida were in a coffee shop yesterday afternoon, when it suddenly started raining and thundering. Then there was a flash of lightning. Miss Yoshida cried,

A, pika-t-to hikatta-wa. (Oh, it flashed.)

to describe the lightning. Mr. Lerner had heard *pikapika* used to describe something brightly shining, but had never heard *pikatto* before.

* * *

Words directly describing manner, called mimesis or mimetic words, are used very frequently in familiar speech. There are numerous words of this kind, and it takes much time to learn them, but a few rules concerning their use will be helpful.

1. One rule is that repeating a sound, as in *pika-pika,* indicates either that the action is repeated or that the state of things remains for some time, as in ぴかぴかに　なる

Yuka-ga pikapika-ni naru made migaita.
(I polished the floor until it shone.)
Pikapika-no shinsha-de shukkin-shite-kita.
(He came to work in his brand-new car — *lit.* in his brightly shining car.)

Recently we can hear the phrase *pikapika-no ichinensei* (shining first-graders) used to describe children who have just entered elementary school; they have everything brand-new, and the special bag they carry on their back — the *randoseru,* the symbol of an elementary school pupil in Japan — is usually shiny.

2. Another rule is that when the action is not repeated, either *ri* is added or a stop sound follows. Miss Yoshida said *pika-t-to hikatta* to describe lightning which flashed just once. She could have used *pikari-to* with the same meaning. If the lightning had flashed several times, she would have used *pikapika-to* instead.

ぴかっと　光つた
ぴかりと　光つた

Thus, *gorogoro* describes something which goes on rolling, and *gorori-to* or *goro-t-to* refers to something rolling just once, as in

1. *Booringu-no booru-ga gorogoro korogatta.*
   (The bowling ball went rolling along.)
2. *Nichiyoobi-wa terebi-no mae-de gorogoro suru-dake-da.*　ごろごろ　する
   (He loafs in front of the TV set on Sundays — *lit.* he lies and rolls.)
3. *Yuube-wa tsukarete, gorori-to yoko-ni natte sugu netchata.*　ごろりと　よこに　なる
   (I was so tired last night that I went asleep the moment I fell into bed.)

To give another set of mimetic words:

1. *Kanojo, kyoo-wa nikoniko-shiteru-ne.*
   (She looks happy today — *lit.* she is smiling happily.)
2. *Sore kiite, kanojo, niko-t-to waratta-yo.*
   (She smiled happily when she heard that.)

. . . shi used to mean 'and what's more'

Mr. Takada and Miss Yoshida were working on packets of papers that had to be sent out soon. While sorting the papers, Miss Yoshida mumbled to herself,

> *Tenki-wa ii-shi . . .*
> 天気は　いいし……
> (The weather is so fine and . . .)

and Mr. Takada immediately agreed. Mr. Lerner did not understand what she had meant. He had understood that *. . . shi* (and what's more) is used to connect two or more phrases or clauses of similar meaning; how could Mr. Takada understand what Miss Yoshida meant from just one phrase?

*   *   *

The particle *shi* is used to combine two or more phrases or clauses that have something in common, as in

> *Hiroi-shi, shizuka-da-shi, ii heya-desu.*
> (It's spacious and quiet; it's a nice room.)
> *Semai-shi, urusai-shi, amari ii heya-ja arimasen.*
> (It's small and noisy; it's not a very good room.)

Two or more phrases or clauses that are combined by *shi* are used to indicate some conclusion. Namely, in the example above, the room being spacious and quiet supports the speaker's high opinion of the room. The room being small and noisy justifies the speaker's low evaluation of the room. In this way, the two or more phrases must serve to support the speaker's judgment.

After the phrases or clauses combined with *shi,* the rest of the sentence can often be left out if the speaker's opinion is easy to understand. For instance, if someone has said

Mono-wa yasui-shi, hito-wa shinsetsu-da-shi . . .
物は　安いし、人は　親切だし……
(**Things are cheap and the people are kind . . .**)

the rest will be something like he likes living in that town or hates to leave it. If someone has said.

Muzukashii-shi, omoshiroku nai-shi . . .
むずかしいし、おもしろく　ないし……
(**It's difficult, and what's more, not interesting . . .**)

he implies that he wants to stop doing something or suggests that you should not start doing it.

Sometimes just one phrase ending in *shi* is enough to imply something. In Miss Yoshida's statement, the weather being fine was likely to be followed by something like wishing the work was not needed in a hurry or was almost over, and she must have been implying that she wished to go out and enjoy the lovely day.

... *hazu* meaning 'it is expected that . . .'

The other day Mr. Lerner and Miss Yoshida had lunch together at a restaurant they had never been to before. The food was all right, but the waiters were blunt and ill-mannered even though there were not many customers there then. When Mr. Lerner commented on the waiters being ill-mannered, Miss Yoshida agreed and said

Kore-ja okyaku-ga konai hazu-desu-ne.
(*lit.* With this, customers cannot be expected to come.)

Mr. Lerner understood that she too was criticizing the restaurant, but did not understand exactly what she meant by *konai hazu.*

* * *

The word *hazu* is used to indicate the speaker's expectation, as in

Tanaka-san-wa sanji-ni kuru hazu-desu.
田中さんは 三時に 来る はずです。
(Mr. Tanaka should come at 3.)
Ano-hito-wa getsuyoo-ni yasumu-kara, kyoo-wa konai hazu-desu.
(Since she takes Mondays off, she should not be here today.)

When using *hazu,* the speaker's expectation is grounded on some concrete information. When one says *sanji-ni kuru-hazu-desu,* one implies that he has an appointment with the person or has some other reason to expect the person to come at 3.

In this respect, *hazu* is different from *beki* or *mono* (should), which are used as in:

68

Gakusee-wa benkyoo-suru beki-da. (Students should study.)

Otoshiyori-wa daiji-ni suru mono-desu.
(You should be kind to old people.)

In such sentences, *hazu* is not used.

Hazu is also used to mean "no wonder" when referring to a particular state of affairs. Miss Yoshida meant, when she said *okyaku-ga konai hazu-desu-ne,* that it is naturally expected that not many customers go to the restaurant — namely, no wonder there were only a few customers there. She was not referring to the future, but to the present state. In this way, one often says something like

Are-ja hito-ni kirawareru hazu-da.
あれじゃ　人に　きらわれる　はずだ。
(No wonder he is not liked by other people.)

when referring to someone's being too strict or easily angered.

Expressing gratitude for someone's help

Mr. Lerner had a lot to do at the office yesterday afternoon. Mr. Takada helped him after his own work was done and they stayed at the office until late. This morning Mr. Lerner wanted to thank him for his help, and started y saying

Kinoo-wa arigatoo-gozaimashita.
(*lit.* Thank you very much for yesterday.)

but he was not sure whether he should say *Tetsudai-o arigatoo-gozaimashita* or *Tetsudatte-kurete, arigatoo-gozaimashita* to mean "Thank you for helping me."

*   *   *

The most basic expression for thanking someone for helping you is to say *Arigatoo-gozaimashita;* to refer to a favor done some time before, one often uses . . . *wa arigatoo-gozaimashita* as in

Yuube-wa arigatoo-gozaimashita.
(*lit.* Thank you very much for yesterday evening.)
Senjitsu-wa arigatoo-gozaimashita.
先日は　ありがとうございました。
(*lit.* Thank you very much for the other day.)

To thank someone for a specific favor, one uses . . . *te-itadaite arigatoo-gozaimashita,* as in

Tetsudatte-itadaite arigatoo-gozaimashita.
(Thank you very much for helping me.)
Iroiro oshiete-itadaite arigatoo-gozaimashita.
(Thank you very much for helping me — *lit.* for

teaching me — said when receiving information or advice.)

In familiar conversation one uses . . . *te-moratte* instead of . . . *te-itadaite* as in

> *Tetsudatte-moratte, arigatoo.*

You could say . . . *te-kudasatte* or . . . *te-kurete* instead of . . . *te-itadaite* or . . . *te-moratte,* but it sounds more appropriate to use the latter; the latter refer to the favor you have received and the former to the other person's action.

It is wrong to use . . . *ta-kara* instead of the . . . *te* form as in *tetsudatte-itadaita-kara* or *tetsudatte-kureta-kara.* It is also wrong to say *tetsudai-o arigatoo-gozaimashita.*

To express your gratitude more positively, you might add an expression such as

> *Okagesama-de hayaku owarimashita.*
> (Thanks to your help, I could finish it quickly.)

Apologizing for being late

Mr. Okada was about 10 minutes late for an appointment with Mr. Lerner yesterday morning. He apologized by repeating

Osoku narimashite, mooshiwake arimasen.
おそく なりまして、申し訳 ありません。
(I'm so sorry to be late — *lit.* I'm late and have no excuse to offer.)

and hurriedly started with the business discussions. After the discussion was over they went out to have lunch together. While having lunch Mr. Lerner discovered that Mr. Okada had had to take his wife to the hospital when she suddenly became ill and that was why he was late. Mr. Lerner wondered why he had not mentioned this when he came.

*　　　*　　　*

When one is late for an appointment, one apologizes by saying

Osoku natte, sumimasen.

or

Osoku narimashite, mooshiwake arimasen.

The second example sounds more polite. And the other person usually replies

Iie.

Sometimes one explains the reason why one was late, and sometimes one does not do so, depending on the individual and the situation. Generally speaking, one explains the reason fully between

72

good friends, but refrains from doing so in polite situations. To be polite, one should spend more time in asking for forgiveness than in explaining the reason; the ratio of explanation to apology is in inverse proportion to the degree of politeness.

It is best to say *sumimasen* or *mooshiwake arimasen* first, and then add the reason briefly, as in

Doomo osoku natte, sumimasen. Chotto kyuuyoo-ga dekimashite.
どうも　おそく　なって、すみません。ちょっと 急用が　できまして。
(I'm sorry I'm late. Some urgent business came up.)
Osoku natte, mooshiwake arimasen. Michi-ga komimashite.
(I'm very sorry I'm late. The traffic was heavy.)

When giving the reason, *kara* should be avoided. If you say something like

Densha-ga okuremashita-kara, osoku narimashita.
(I'm late because the train was late.)

it will sound as if you were asserting that your being late is amply justified and you have no need to feel sorry.

Accepting an invitation

Miss Yoshida asked Mr. Lerner if he was going to join the others at the picnic on the coming Saturday. He wanted to join them, so he answered

Hai, ikimashoo.

meaning "Yes, I will go." But he wondered if he should have used such expressions as

Ikoo-to omoimasu.
or
Iku tsumori-desu.

*　　　*　　　*

To indicate one's intention of doing something in the future there are several expressions that can be used.

When one is certain about the future, one uses the . . . *masu* form, as in

Ikimasu.
行きます。
(I will go.)

When you are accepting an invitation to go somewhere, you should say *Ikimasu* rather than *Ikimashoo. Ikimashoo* is used either when you invite someone to go out with you or when you have decided on going after thinking about it for some time. Replying *Ikimashoo* to an invitation can sound condescending, implying "All right. I have decided to go after all." Therefore one should avoid saying *Ikimashoo* when one has to be polite.

. . .*oo*/. . . *yoo-to omoimasu* is used when you

are especially conscious of your intentions. It is used as in

Ashita ikoo-to omoimasu. (I intend to go tomorrow.)
Yomoo yomoo-to omoinagara mada yonde-imasen.
(I have been meaning to read it, but haven't been able to do so.)

. . . *tsumori-desu* is used when one is especially conscious of one's plans, as in

Konshuu-juu-ni owaru tsumori-desu.
(I plan to finish it by the end of this week.)
Sono tsumori-datta-n-da-kedo . . .
(I was planning to do so, but . . .)

When you have to indicate your plans or intentions precisely, you should use . . . *tsumori-desu* or . . . *ool . . . yoo-to omoimasu,* but to indicate that you will accept an invitation, . . . *masu* is most appropriate because it definitely shows that you are ready to do it.

. . . *to itte-mo* used for qualification

Mr. Lerner and his colleagues were talking about their holidays yesterday afternoon when Mr. Kato, who usually stays home during vacations, said

Boku, gaikoku-e itte-kita-yo. (I went abroad.)

Everybody looked surprised. Then, as if wanting to enjoy another surprise, Mr. Kato added

To itte-mo, Honkon-da-kedo-ne.
(However, it was Hong Kong.)

Mr. Lerner understood what Mr. Kato meant, but he was not sure about this usage of . . . *to itte-mo* (*lit.* even though I say. . .).

*   *   *

To itte-mo is used to qualify what has been said immediately before, as in

Ano-hito, yoku hatarakimasu-yo. To itte-mo, Yoshida-san-niwa kanaimasen-ga.
(He is a hard worker. However, he does not work as hard as Miss Yoshida.)
Kinoo-wa isogashikatta. To-itte-mo, hirugohan-ga taberarenai hodo-ja nakatta-kedo.
(I was busy yesterday, but not so busy as to have to do without lunch.)

Sometimes . . .*to itte-mo* is used to connect two phrases instead of two sentences, as in

Isogashii-to itte-mo, hirugohan-ga taberarenai hodo-ja nakatta.

Kane-ga nai-to itte-mo, koohii-ga nomenai wake-ja arimasen.

(I don't have much money, but it's not so bad that I can't have some coffee.)

Ryokoo-ni iku-to itte-mo, honno nisannichi-desu.

旅行に 行くと いっても、ほんの 二三日です。

(I'm going on a trip, but it's just for a couple of days.)

What comes after . . .*to itte-mo* usually qualifies what has been said before. Mr. Kato surprised his listeners with the announcement that he had been abroad, and then revealed that he had not gone very far.

To be polite, . . . *to iimashite-mo* or . . .*to mooshimashite-mo* is used, and in familiar conversation . . .*to ittatte* is also used.

Nihongo-o naraimashita. To iimashite-mo, hon-no shoho-dake-desu.

(I learned Japanese, but just at the beginning level.)

Tetsudatte-kureta-to itta-tte, honno chotto-dake-da.

手つだってくれたと いったって、ほんの ちょっ とだけだ。

(He helped me all right, but only a little bit.)

Uses of *tokoro*

While explaining a project of his to Mr. Mori, the company director, Mr. Takada said

Moo ichido shirabete-mimashita tokoro, hiyoo-ga daibu kakaru yoo-de. . .
(When I examined it again, I found that it seems to cost quite a bit.)

Mr. Lerner understood but was confused about the use of the word *tokoro*, which seems to be used in various ways.

* * *

The word *tokoro* (*lit.* place) is used to refer to a situation; *ii tokoro* means "the right moment" and *oisogashii tokoro* means "while you are busy," as in

Choodo ii tokoro-e irasshaimashita.
(You've come at exactly the right moment.)
Oisogashii tokoro-o sumimasen.
おいそがしい　ところを　すみません。
(I'm sorry to trouble you when you're busy.)

When it is used with the present form of a verb, it means "be about to . . ." as in

Kore-kara dekakeru tokoro-desu.
(I'm about to go out.)

And when it is used with the . . .*te-iru* form of a verb, it means "while . . . ing" as in

Ima junbi-shite-iru tokoro-desu-kara, chotto omachi-kudasai.

(I'm now preparing it, so would you please wait a moment?)

When *tokoro* is used with the *ta* form of a verb, it means "have/has just. . ." as in

Ima tsuita tokoro-desu. (I have just arrived.)
Choodo dekiagatta tokoro-desu.
(It has just been completed.)

In Mr. Takada's sentence, . . .*ta tokoro* is different from all of the uses mentioned above; it is used to connect two clauses, meaning "when," as in

Omoikitte onegai-shite-mita tokoro, kokoroyoku hikiukete-kudasaimashita.
(When I went ahead and asked him, he readily agreed to do it.)

In this usage, . . .*ta tokoro* resembles . . .*tara*. In the above example, as well as in Mr. Takada's sentence, . . .*tara* can replace . . .*ta tokoro* without changing the meaning. However, . . .*ta tokoro* sounds more formal, and is used in polite speech or public speaking.

. . . te-mitara meaning 'and found that'

Miss Yoshida wanted to buy a ticket for a concert by a famous foreign singer she liked very much. When Mr. Lerner asked her if she had bought a ticket, she said

Iie, itte-mitara urikire-deshita.
行ってみたら、売り切れでした。
(No. When I went to buy one, I found that all the tickets were sold out.)

Mr. Lerner thought that he would have said something like

Kai-ni itta toki urikireta koto-o mitsukemashita.
or
Kai-ni itta toki urikire-da-to wakarimashita.

and wondered if *wakaru* or *mitsukeru* were wrong here.

* * *

When you have done something and seen the result, the expression *. . . te-mitara* (or *. . . te-miru-to*) is commonly used rather than *wakaru* or *mitsukeru*. For instance,

Yotte-mitara rusu-deshita.
寄ってみたら　るすでした。
(I dropped by his home and found that he was out.)
Yonde-miru-to omoshiroi-desu-yo.
(If you read it, you will find it interesting.)
Kaette-mitara tomodachi-ga matte-imashita.
(I returned home and found my friend waiting for me.)

80

In Miss Yoshida's sentence, *urikire-deshita* can be replaced by *urikirete-imashita* as in

Itte-mitara urikirete-imashita.

but *urikiremashita* is not used because you need an expression indicating a state rather than an action.
. . .*te-miru* is different from . . . *(y)oo-to suru* (try to, be about to); while . . . *(y)oo-to suru* refers to an attempt to do something. . . . *te-miru* indicates that you do something with an interest in the result. Thus

Tabeyoo-to shimashita-ga taberaremasen-deshita.

means that you tried to eat something but you couldn't. On the other hand saying

Tabete-mimashita-ga oishiku arimasen-deshita.

means that you ate something to see what it would taste like, and found that it was not very good.

Phonetic changes in rapid speech
(1) the dropping of the 'i' sound

Miss Yoshida was talking with a young woman colleague yesterday afternoon; she talked about a photo and said

Ja, ato-de motte-ku-wa.
(Then I will bring it to you later.)

Mr. Lerner realized that the *i* sound is dropped not only in *iru* but also in *iku*.

* * *

In rapid speech, the *i* sound is often left out. The most common case is in the expression . . .*te-iru*, as in

Ashita matte-masu.
あした　待ってます。
(I will be waiting for you tomorrow.)
Ima ocha-o nonde-ru tokoro-desu.
(I am having some tea now.)

The *i* sound is also dropped in *iku* when it is used with other verbs; the *i* in *itta* (said, went) is also dropped in rapid speech.

Dare-ga motte-ku-no.
だれが　持ってくの。
(Who is going to take it there?)
Dandan atsuku natte-ku-deshoo-ne.
(It will get warmer and warmer.)
Kinoo motte-tta hazu-da.
(I'm sure I took it there yesterday.)
Kare, nante-tta-no.
(What did he say?)

The *i* sound is also dropped in *irassharu* as in

Itte-rasshai.
行ってらつしやい。
(Good-bye, said to someone leaving the house
— *lit.* Please go and come back.)
Asoko-de matte-rasshaimasu-yo.
(He is waiting there.)

In very rapid, familiar speech, the *i* sound is
also left out in the phrase . . . *ni naru*, as in

Sanji-n nattara oshiete.
三時ん　なつたら　教えて。
(Tell me when it's 3 o'clock.)
Muri-o suru-to byooki-n naru-yo.
(If you overwork, you'll become sick.)

When the *i* sound is dropped several times in
one sentence, it is difficult to understand the
meaning.

Sanji-n nattara motte-ku-tte-tta-yo.
(He said he would take it at 3.)

is a contracted version of

Sanji-ni nattara motte-iku-to itta-yo.

83

. . .*yasui* (easy to) and . . .*nikui* (hard to)

Miss Yoshida seemed quite busy yesterday afternoon. She went to Mr. Takada and asked him to help her. He said he would, but suggested that she might ask Mr. Hayashi instead. She apologized for troubling him, and added

Hayashi-san-wa nandaka tanominikui-kara.
(Somehow Mr. Hayashi is difficult to ask.)

Mr. Lerner heard this, and was interested to see that the suffix . . .*nikui* can be used with human beings, too.

* * *

The suffix . . .*nikui* is used with the stem of a verb, and adds the meaning of "difficult to. . .," as in

Kono kaban-wa mochinikui.
(This suitcase is hard to carry.)
Ji-ga chiisakute yominikui-desu.
字が 小さくて 読みにくいです。
(The print is small and difficult to read.)
Michi-ga wakarinikui-desu-kara, goannai-shimashoo.
(Since it is hard to locate, I will go with you.)

The antonym of . . .*nikui* is . . .*yasui*.

Ji-ga ookikute yomiyasui-desu.
字が 大きくて 読みやすいです。
(The print is big and easy to read.)
Wakariyasuku setsumee-shite-kuremashita.
(He explained in a way that we could easily understand.)

84

Whether some action is . . .*yasui* (easy to do)
. . . *nikui* (hard to do) is judged from the viewpoint of the speaker. Therefore, *Hayashi-san-wa tanominikui* means that the speaker finds it difficult to ask Mr. Hayashi to do something for him; it does not mean that Mr. Hayashi finds it difficult to ask someone to help him.

One often talks about others in this way as in

tsukiainikui hito (a person who is difficult to associate with)

wakarinikui hito (a person who is difficult to understand)

hanashiyasui hito (a person who is easy to talk to, a friendly person)

Phonetic changes in rapid speech (2) the dropping of the 'o' sound

When Mr. Lerner was having coffee with Mr. Takada during their break, Mr. Takada complained about his health, saying

Koko-n toko, doomo tsukareyasukute.
ここん　とこ
(I tire easily these days.)

This sort of complaint is rather common among the Japanese, but Mr. Lerner was interested in the phrase *koko-n toko*, in which the o sound has been dropped.

*   *   *

The o sound in the particle *no* is very often dropped in rapid speech. *Watashi-no* (my) often becomes *watashi-n* and *boku-no* (my, used by men) becomes *boku-n* when followed by a noun, *desu* or *da*.

Watashi-n toko-wa kazoku-ga sukunai-kara, kore-
わたしん　とこ
de juubun-desu.
(My family is small, so this is enough for us.)
Boku-n chi-de yaroo-yo.
ぼくん　ち
(Let's do it at my house.)
Kore, boku-n-da-yo.
(This is mine.)

In the same way, . . . *no-desu* (it is that . . .) is usually pronounced . . . *n-desu* in familiar conversation as in

Ima jikan-ga nai-n-desu.
(I don't have time for it now.)

Doo shita-n-desu-ka.
(What's the matter?)

Also, the word *tokoro* is often pronounced *toko*
with the *r* sound as well the *o* sound being dropped;
thus *koko-no tokoro* (recently) is pronounced
koko-n toko in rapid speech.

And the particle *o* is often left out, as in

Ocha nonde-kara ikimashoo.
(Let's go after having some tea.)
Moo shigoto yamemasu.
もう　仕事　やめます。
(I'm going to stop working now.)

In kanji compounds plus *suru*, such as
benkyoo-o suru (to study) or *choosa-o suru* (to in-
vestigate), the particle *o* is often dropped, as in

Moo sukoshi choosa shite-kara kimemashoo.
(Let's make a decision after investigating it a
little more.)

But when the compound is followed by a modifier,
the particle *o* should not be omitted.

Juubunna choosa-o suru koto-ga hitsuyoo-desu.
(It is necessary to make a full investigation.)

Hai and *Soo-desu*
('Yes' and 'That's right')

Mr. Lerner was receiving instructions on a project he was engaged in from Mr. Mori, the director of the company. Mr. Takada was with him. When Mr. Mori paused while giving his instructions, Mr. Lerner said

Soo-desu. (Right.)

to convey that he had agreed so far. But later Mr. Takada said that he should have said

Hai.

instead of *Soo-desu* while listening to a superior. Mr. Lerner did not know that *Soo-desu* is less polite than *Hai*.

* * *

Soo-desu means "That is so," "That is right," and can be used to express one's agreement. It is all right to use it when you are indicating agreement to a factual question, such as

Shitsuree-desu-ga, Tanaka-san-desu-ka.
(Excuse me. Are you Mr. Tanaka?)
Kono michi-o iku-to eki-ni demasu-ka.
(Can I go to the station by taking this road?)

But when you have to show respect to the person you are talking with, it is better to say *Hai* rather than *Soo-desu*, even when you are indicating agreement with him. Sometimes *Hai* and *Soo-desu* are used together as in

Hai, soo-desu.

はい、そうです。

The expression *Hai* does not just indicate agreement but also conveys the speaker's polite attitude, or willingness to cooperate with or obey the other person. Thus, *Hai, soo-desu* can be paraphrased as "I'm glad to answer your question; the answer is yes." Therefore sometimes *Hai* is used together with negative information. For example, if someone asks Mrs. Yamada on the phone

Moshimoshi, goshujin irasshaimasu-ka.
(Hello, is Mr. Yamada home?)

she is likely to answer

Hai, orimasen-ga.
(Sorry, he's not home — *lit*. Yes, he is not home.)
or
Hai. Ima chotto dete-orimasu.
(Sorry, he is out — *lit*. Yes, he is out.)

89

Komarimasu used in a reprimand

Yesterday afternoon Mr. Lerner went to the office of Mr. Mori, the director of the company, to talk with him about a project of his. When he entered, he heard Mr. Mori admonishing his young secretary about some sort of negligence, saying

Ki-o tsukete-kurenai-to komaru-yo.
(You should be more careful — *lit*. If you are not careful, I will be troubled.)

Mr. Lerner realized then that the expression *komaru* is used in the case of a reprimand like this, and not only in complaints.

*   *   *

The phrase *komaru* or *komarimasu*, which literally means "I will be troubled," is also used to mean "something is not good" or "something does not work," as in

Ashita-wa chotto komarimasu.
あしたは　ちょっと　困ります。
(Tomorrow will not be good for me.)
Sore-wa komaru. (That won't do.)

When it is used together with . . . *nai-to/. . . nakereba* (if you don't . . .), it means "you should . . ."

Hayaku shite-kurenai-to komarimasu.
早く　してくれないと　困ります。
(Please do it quickly — *lit*. If you don't do it quickly, I'll be troubled.)
Machigai-no nai yoo-ni shite-kurenakereba komarimasu.

(You must try not to make any mistakes.)

The expression . . . *nai-to/. . . nakereba komarimasu* can be used either for reprimands or requests; whether it is used for a reprimand or for a request can be judged from the context.

If *komarimasu* is used with . . . *suru-to/. . . shite-wa* (if you do . . .), it means "you shouldn't . . ." or "please don't . . ." as in

Sonna koto-o sareru-to komaru-yo.
(You shouldn't do that — *sareru* indicates that the speaker suffers from someone doing something.)

Sometimes this expression is used for a polite reprimand, such as when someone has offered one an expensive gift or too much service.

Sonna koto-made shite-itadaite-wa komatte-shimaimasu.
(I wish you hadn't gone to so much trouble.)

When you are actually troubled, . . . *te-iru* is used, as in

Shorui-ga mitsukaranakute komatte-imasu.
(I don't know what to do; I can't find the document.)

The use of the imperative
in indirect speech

Yesterday morning Miss Yoshida looked very tired. When Mr. Lerner asked her about it, she said that she had been so busy at the office and gone home so late that her mother was worried and had even suggested that she quit work. She said

Kaisha-nanka yamete-shimae-tte yuu-n-desu-yo.
(She said I should quit the company.)

and added that she would not do so.

Mr. Lerner seldom heard the plain imperative form used at the office, and wondered if women also use it in speech.

* * *

Plain imperative forms like *Ike* (Go!) or *Yamero* (Stop!) are not often used in conversation. This form is used in (1) very familiar speech among men, (2) signs and (3) quoted speech.

Close male friends often use this form between themselves as in

Hayaku koi-yo. (Come quickly.)
早く 来いよ。
Joodan-wa yamero. (Stop joking.)
Chotto kashite-kure. (Lend it to me a little while.)

In such speech too, very often some expression of intimacy like *yo* or . . . *te-kure* is added, because using the imperative form by itself can sound blunt.

In written signs, the plain imperative is often used because of its brevity and strong impression.

Tomare. (Stop!)
止まれ。

For the negative imperative, *na* is added to the dictionary form.

Kiken. Te-o fureru-na.
危険。手を　ふれるな。
(Danger. Don't touch.)

Finally, in polite speech, the plain imperative form is used in quotation, as in Miss Yoshida's remark. Her mother must have used some other expression like

Yamete-shimainasai-yo. (Quit, will you?)
or
Yamete-shimattara doo? (Why don't you quit?)

Miss Yoshida changed this into the plain imperative form in quoting it. In the same way, one often uses this form when conveying someone's order, as in

Shachoo-ga kuji-ni koi-to osshaimashita-node. . .
社長が　九時に　来いと　おつしやいましたので。
(The company director told me to come at 9.)
Kore-o ichiman-en-de ure-tte ossharu-n-desu-ka. Muri-desu-yo.
(Are you asking me to sell this for ¥10,000? That's impossible.)

Men's & women's sentence endings in familiar conversation

Since Mr. Lerner has been working for the same company for several years and knows his colleagues well, he sometimes wonders if he should use familiar speech with them. Yesterday afternoon when Miss Yoshida, talking about a movie with her colleagues, said

Totemo yokatta-wa. (It was very good.)

he tried to reinforce her statement, by saying

Keshiki-mo kiree-yo. (The scenery is good, too.)

Everybody laughed, and some praised his imitation of women's sentence endings, which he had not intended.

* * *

In familiar speech men and women often use different sentence endings. The most important difference is that in men's speech, nouns and quasi-adjectives (adjective-verbs or *-na* adjectives) are followed by *dane* or *dayo*, while in women's speech they are followed by *ne* or *yo*. This can be called Group I.

Group I

men	Women
Ame-dane/dayo.	*Ame-ne/yo.*
雨だね	雨ね
(It's raining.)	
Kiree-dane/dayo.	*Kiree-ne/yo.*
きれいだね	きれいね
(It's pretty.)	

And true adjectives (or -*i* adjectives) and verbs are immediately followed by *ne* or *yo* in men's speech, while they are followed by *wane* or *wayo* in women's speech. This is Group II.

Group II

men	women
Omoshiroi-ne/yo.	*Omoshiroi-wane/wayo.*
(It's interesting.)	
Iku-ne/yo.	*Iku-wane/wayo.*
行くよ	行くわよ
(I'm going.)	

The negative forms of verbs, adjectives and quasi-adjectives are like true adjectives; they belong to Group II.

Group II

men	women
Ikanai-ne/yo.	*Ikanai-wane/wayo.*
行かないね	行かないわね
(I'm not going.)	
Ikanakatta-ne/yo.	*Ikanakatta-wane/wayo.*
(I didn't go.)	
Yoku nai-ne/yo.	*Yoku nai-wane/wayo.*
(It's not good.)	
Yoku nakatta-ne/yo.	*Yoku nakatta-wane/wayo.*
(It wasn't good.)	
Kiree-ja nai-ne/yo.	*Kiree-ja nai-wane/wayo.*
(It isn't pretty.)	
Kiree-ja nakatta-ne/yo.	*Kiree-ja nakatta-wane/wayo.*
(It wasn't pretty.)	

The various uses of *hai*

While Mr. Lerner was visiting the Takadas yesterday afternoon, there was a telephone call that Mrs. Takada answered. It was apparently from a salesman, and Mrs. Takada said

Uchi-wa irimasen. Hai. (We don't want it.)

and hung up. Mr. Lerner noticed that she had used *hai* to imply that she did not want to talk any more; he wondered just how many ways this word can be used.

*　　　*　　　*

Hai has several uses in actual conversation. First, like the English "yes," it is used to indicate agreement, as in

A: *Goshujin-wa otaku-desu-ka.*
(Is your husband home?)
B: *Hai.* (Yes, he is.)

Another use is to indicate that you have understood what you have heard, as in

A: *Goshujin-ni ome-ni kakaritai-n-desu-ga.*
(I'd like to see your husband.)
B: *Hai. Ainiku ima orimasen-ga.*
(I see. I'm sorry but he's out now.)

In this case *hai* does not mean "yes"; it corresponds to "I see" or "I understand."

This usage is seen in *aizuchi,* response words, as in the following conversation.

A: *Kyoo-wa atsukute shigoto-ga dekinai-n-de. . .*
(It was so hot today that I couldn't work.)
B: *Hai.* ……はい……
A: *Hayaku uchi-e Kaette yasunde-ita-n-desu-ga. . .*
(I went home early and was resting.)
B: *Hai.* ……はい……
A: *Doomo shigoto-ga ki-ni natte kaisha-e modorimashita.*
(I couldn't stop thinking about work and went back to the office.)

B's answer *hai* is *aizuchi* and is used to mean "I understand so far. Please go on."

Another use is to imply that you want to terminate the conversation, as Mrs. Takada did. One often says

Wakarimashita, hai.
わかりました、はい。

to show that one has completely understood and does not want any further explanation.

Hai is also used to call someone's attention to an action, as in

Hai, hajimemashoo. (All right. Let's start now.)
Hai, soko-no hito, chotto migi-e yotte-kudasai.
(Say, would you there please move over to the right? — said by a photographer.)

Phonetic changes in rapid speech
(3) *nakucha* & *nakya*

Yesterday was a busy day for everyone at the office; Miss Yoshida seemed particularly busy. At about 4:30, she looked up at the clock on the wall and said to herself

Saa, isoganakucha. (Well, I must hurry.)

Then Mr. Takada also said,

Soo-da. Boku-mo isoide kore yaranakya.
(Right. I have to hurry with this, too.)

Mr. Lerner understood what they meant, but he still found it difficult to use such contracted forms as . . .*nakucha* and . . .*nakya* himself.

*   *   *

The form . . .*kute-wa* (if one does . . ./if it isn't . . .) is often contracted as . . .*kucha;* the negative form is contracted as . . . *nakucha.*

Konna-ni atsukucha shigoto-ga dekinai.
(One cannot work when it is as hot as this.)
Isoganakucha ma-ni aimasen-yo.
急がなくちゃ　間に　合いませんよ。
(If you don't hurry, you won't be in time.)

Consequently, the expression . . .*nakute-wa narimasen/ikemasen* (one must . . .) often becomes . . . *nakucha narimasen/ikemasen* in rapid speech, and the last part *narimasen/ikemasen* is often left out.

Isoganakucha.
急がなくちゃ。

(I must hurry.)

Moo oitoma-shinakucha.

(I must leave now — said when visiting someone.)

Another expression ... *nakereba nari-masen/ikemasen* (one must . . .) is often pronounced as ... *nakya* in rapid speech.

Isoganakya.

急がなきゃ。

(I must hurry.)

Moo oitoma-shinakya.

(I must leave now.)

... *kereba* is contracted as ... *kya* as well as *kerya;* in the latter case ... *nakereba* becomes ... *nakerya,* as in *Isoganakerya.*

Of these three contractions, ... *nakucha* is the most commonly used in Tokyo, especially by young people. All of these contracted forms are common in Tokyo, while they are not in common use in the Kansai district.

Hidden sentence subjects
(1) a continued topic

Mr. Lerner and Miss Yoshida were talking yesterday when Mr. Takada returned from lunch and asked if Mr. Okada had come while he was out. She answered

Ee. Kore-o motte-irasshaimashita. Okaeri-ni nat-tara owatashi-shite-kudasai-tte.

and handed him a packet of papers. Mr. Lerner noticed that none of her sentences had a subject, and wondered if this type of omission couldn't cause misunderstanding.

* * *

Sentence subjects are not usually verbally expressed in Japanese but are indicated by some other means, and this seldom causes any misunderstanding. One such means is the rule that when the topic stays the same it is not mentioned again. In the case of Miss Yoshida, she did not repeat *Okada-san* because Mr. Takada had mentioned this in his question. Thus, in

Kore-o motte-irasshaimashita.

the subject is Mr. Odaka, and it means "He brought this."

In her second sentence, since she did not start a new subject, Mr. Okada is still the subject. The last part, . . . *tte,* means "someone said. . ." and this "someone" is naturally Mr. Okada. *Okaeri-ni. . .te-kudasai* was Mr. Okada's statement. Thus, the second sentence means "He asked me to hand this to you when you returned."

In the same way, the subject is left out when the speaker continues referring to the same topic, as in the following conversation.

A: *Kinoo Yamada-san-ni atta-soo-desu-ne.*
(I heard you met Mr. Yamada yesterday.)
B: *Ee. Genki-deshita-yo. Kondo kaisha-o yamete, kissaten-o hajimeta-node, isogashii-soo-desu.*
(Yes. He was fine. He said that he had quit his job and started running a coffee shop that keeps him quite busy.)

It would be strange if B repeated the subject as in

B: *Ee. Watashi-wa Yamada-san-ni aimashita. Yamada-san-wa genki-deshita-yo. Kare-wa kaisha-o yamete. . .*

When the topic is changed, however, it is mentioned to avoid misunderstanding, as in

B: *Ee. Genki-deshita-yo. Demo, okusan-ga nyuuin-shita-soo-desu.*
(Yes. He was fine, but his wife had been hospitalized, he said.)

Hidden sentence subjects
(2) polite terms

Mr. Lerner visited Professor Takahashi the other day. Mrs. Takahashi asked him about Margaret, his sister. When he mentioned that she wants to come to Japan someday, Mrs. Takahashi said

Kochira-ni irassharu uchi-ni oide-ni naru-to ii-desu-ne.
こちらに　いらっしゃる　うちに　おいでに　なる
と　いいですね。

He understood what she meant, but again he was surprised to notice that she did not use any sentence subject at all.

* * *

One means of indicating a sentence subject without verbally mentioning it is through the use of polite terms. Polite terms are used only for the second and third persons, excluding the possibility of referring to the speaker himself.

In Mrs. Takahashi's sentence,

kochira-ni irassharu uchi-ni

can mean either "while you are here" or "while she is here," but from the context it was clear that it referred to Mr. Lerner being in Japan. Thus, this phrase means "while you are here."

oide-ni naru

can refer either to "your coming" or "her coming," but from the context it is clear that it referred to her coming. Thus by *oide-ni naru-to ii-desu-ne,*

Mrs. Takahashi meant "I hope she comes — *lit.* it will be good if she comes."

The use of humble expressions can also indicate sentence subjects, because they can only refer to the speaker himself. Thus, a dressmaker will say to her customer

> *Matte-irassharu aida-ni onaoshi-shimasu.*
> (I will fix it for you while you wait.)

In this sentence, *matte-irassharu* is a polite expression used to refer to the second person, and *onaoshi-shimasu,* a humble form, is used to refer to the speaker. In the same way,

> *Otodoke-shita toki, haratte-kudasaimashita.*

can mean either
"He/ She paid me when I delivered it."
or
"You paid me when I delivered it."
depending on the situation.

Hidden sentence subjects
(3) situational

Mr. Lerner visited the Takadas last Saturday afternoon and was having tea with them, when a neighbor came by. She brought along a magazine that Mrs. Takada had wanted to see. After she left, Mr. Takada said

Shinsetsuna hito-dane.
(She's a kind person.)

and Mrs. Takada agreed saying

Ee. Itsumo iroirona koto-o oshiete-kureru-no.
(Yes. She always helps me with various information.)

Mr. Lerner noticed that neither Mr. Takada nor Mrs. Takada used the neighbor's name or *ano-hito* (she).

*   *   *

When the topic of the conversation is obvious from the situation, it is not verbally mentioned in Japanese. Mr. Takada could have said

Satoo-san-wa shinsetsuna hito-dane.
or
Ano-hito-wa shinsetsu-dane.

but usually the subject is not mentioned, unless it is being particularly emphasized. And since the topic remained the same in Mrs. Takada's sentences, she did not mention it either.

In the same way, when two people see a dish of food in front of them on the table, they will say something like

A: *Oishisoo-desu-ne.* おいしそうですね。
(It looks good.)
B: *Ee, soo-desu-ne.* ええ、そうですね。
(Yes, it does.)

They will not say something like

A: *Kono ryoori-wa oishisoo-desu-ne.*
(This dish looks good.)
B: *Ee. Kore-wa oishisoo-desu-ne.*
(Yes. This looks good.)

unless they want to emphasize that one particular
dish looks better than others.

Sometimes the subject of a sentence cannot be
understood without a knowledge of the situation.
For instance the subject in the following series of
sentences is determined only by the situation.

A: *Osoi-desu-ne.*
B: *Ee. Dooshite konna-ni osoi-n-deshoo-ne.*
A: *Doo shimashoo. Moo sukoshi machimashoo-
ka.*
B: *Soo-desu-ne. Soo shimashoo.*

The two people could be waiting for a bus or for a
person, wondering why it/he is so late and deciding
to wait a little while longer.

...*wa* used to indicate contrast

Mr. Kato, the section chief, was planning a study trip over the weekend and asked Mr. Lerner and several other people if they were going. Everybody answered

Ikimasu. (I'm going.)

When his turn came, Mr. Lerner inadvertently said

Watashi-wa...
わたしは……

and paused before saying *ikimasu.* To his surprise, everybody seemed to think that he was not going before they heard the last part of the sentence.

* * *

When indicating one's intentions or plans, *watashi-wa* is usually left out; therefore Mr. Lerner's colleagues just said *Ikimasu* rather than *Watashi-wa ikimasu.* Inserting *watashi-wa* in such a case means that the speaker is different from the others. Thus, when Mr. Lerner got as far as *watashi-wa...* his listeners naturally thought that he was not going while everybody else was.

He would have been understood correctly if he had said

Watashi-mo...

instead of *watashi-wa...*

Watashi-wa ikimasu would also be appropriate if the speaker was going and no one else was.

In this way, a sentence subject with *wa* inserted

when mentioning the subject is unnecessary places the subject in contrast with others.

To give another example, suppose two people are discussing the schedules of other people before deciding the date of a meeting.

A: *Yamada-san-wa?* (What about Mr. Yamada?)

B: *Ii soo-desu.* (He says it's okay.)

A: *Kawakami-san-wa?* (Mr. Kawakami?)

B: *Ii-to itte-mashita.* (He said it's all right.)

A: *Mori-san-mo?* (Mr. Mori, too?)
森さんも？

B: *Mori-san-wa. . .* (As for Mr. Mori. . .)
森さんは……

In this case, speaker A would have known that Mr. Mori couldn't go without hearing the rest of B's answer, although he might have confirmed this as in the following exchange.

A: *Dame-desu-ka?* (He can't?)

B: *Ee.* (He can't.)

Exchanging complaints

It was very hot when Mr. Okada came in for business discussions yesterday afternoon. While wiping off his forehead he said

Koo atsukute-wa doo shiyoo-mo arimasen-ne.
(When it is as hot as this, we can do nothing about it.)

Mr. Lerner almost said, "Yes, there is something you can do. Why don't you take off your coat and loosen your tie?", but the next moment he remembered that this was a kind of greeting and said

Ee, atsui-desu-ne. Atsukute komarimasu-ne.
(*lit.* Yes, it's hot, isn't it? It's so hot we don't know what to do.)

Mr. Takada smiled at Mr. Lerner as if to say "You've learned it."

*　　　*　　　*

It is common for people to comment on the weather by way of opening a conversation, and most often the Japanese seem to complain about the weather being unpleasant. Especially in summer, complaints about the heat are frequently exchanged, as in:

Atsukute tamarimasen-ne.
暑くて　たまりませんね。
(*lit.* It's so hot that we can't stand it.)
Atsukute iya-desu-ne.
(*lit.* It's hot and disagreeable.)
Atsukute kanaimasen-ne.
(*lit.* It's so hot that we can't cope with it.)

Toward the end of summer, people will complain about the late arrival of autumn.

Itsu-made-mo atsukute, iya-ni narimasu-ne.
いつまでも　暑くて、いやに　なりますね。
(It is still so hot that we don't like it.)

Similar expressions are also used about the cold. And complaints can be heard not only about the weather, but also about crowded trains, high prices and various other things when two Japanese meet.

It may seem as if the Japanese are particularly fond of complaining and do so for the mere sake of complaining, but actually these complaints are used to indicate that both the speaker and listener share the same hardship and sympathize with each other. In short, exchanging complaints in this way is actually exchanging sympathy for the purpose of confirming good relations.

Indirect requests

When leaving after business discussions with Mr. Lerner and Mr. Takada yesterday afternoon, Mr. Okada started talking about a friend. He said that a friend of his in Kyushu was coming up to Tokyo and since this was his first visit to Tokyo, he would have to go to the airport to meet him and help him do the sights. Mr. Lerner was wondering why he was talking about this friend at such length, when Mr. Takada said,

Taihen-desu-ne. De, sore, itsu-desu-ka.
たいへんですね。で、それ、いつですか。
(That's tough, isn't it? And when will he come?)

Then Mr. Okada, looking relieved, said that it would fall on the day of their next meeting and that he wondered if the meeting could be postponed. Mr. Lerner wondered if this couldn't have been stated more directly.

*　　　*　　　*

Yes, Mr. Odaka could have said straightforwardly

Jitsu-wa Kyuushuu-kara tomodachi-ga kuru-node, kondo-no kaigi-wa nobashite-itadakenai-deshoo-ka.
(As a matter of fact, since my friend is coming up from Kyushu, can I have the next meeting postponed?)

This would save time. But sometimes people prefer indirect development of a conversation, especially when making a request that will inconvenience the

110

other person. And on the listener's side, it is regarded as good to be attentive and sense what the other person really wants. Mr. Takada did this and made it easier for Mr. Okada to make his request by asking him when his friend was coming.

There are several ways to judge whether the speaker is just talking or trying to make an indirect request. One is to pay attention to the tone of the speaker; when aiming at a request, he will sound as if he is continuing with his talk indefinitely rather than concluding it quickly. Another hint is that he makes comments, by way of complaining, like the following:

Sore-de, chotto komatte-irun-desu-ga. . .
(So, I'm a little inconvenienced by it.)
Doomo umaku ikanakute. . .
(Somehow it doesn't go well.)
Doo shiyoo-ka-to omotte-iru tokoro-desu-kedo. . .
どう　しようかと　思っている　ところですけど…
(I'm wondering what to do.)

Sounds difficult to hear
(1) short and long vowels

When Mr. Lerner came out of the office after work yesterday evening, Mr. Takada was waiting for him at the door and said

Chotto iitai koto-ga aru-n-da-kedo.

Mr. Lerner thought that he was suffering from pain of some kind and asked *Doko-ga itai-n-desu-ka* (*lit.* What part of your body hurts?). Mr. Takada looked puzzled and after a few exchanges, they realized that Mr. lerner had misunderstood what Mr. Takada said. Mr. Takada meant "I have something I'd like to tell you," but Mr. Lerner thought that he had used the phrase *itai* (painful) instead of *iitai* (want to say).

* * *

The distinction between short and long vowels often causes difficulty for foreigners in the aural comprehension of Japanese. There are several pairs of similar-sounding words that are distinguished only by the length of the vowel, such as

    shujin (husband, master) *shuujin* (prisoner)
    koko (here)   *kookoo* (high school)
    ojisan (uncle)   *ojiisan* (grandfather)

When pronouncing a long vowel, you should try to pronounce it as two syllables rather than as a long single vowel. Namely, when pronouncing the word *kookoo,* say it as a four-syllable word

    ko-o-ko-o

rather than as a two-syllable word containing two long vowels — *ko-ko*. When saying *iitai* (I want to say), try to pronounce it as

i-i-ta-i.

But when you try to distinguish short vowels from long ones, you should know that long vowels are not twice as long as short ones in natural speech; they are usually pronounced 60 to 70 percent longer rather than 100 percent longer. Therefore it requires some practice in distinguishing long and short vowels by ear. It is recommended that you have sets of words like the following pronounced by a Japanese and practice listening to them. (You can make use of recorded tapes, too.)

soko (bottom)	*sooko* (warehouse)
obasan (aunt)	*obaasan* (grandmother)
おばさん	おばあさん
toku (gain)	*tooku* (distant place)
yoji (4 o'clock)	*yooji* (business)
４時	用事
oo (king)	*oo-oo* (sometimes)

Sounds difficult to hear
(2) soft consonants

Mr. Lerner received a telephone call from Mrs. Okada, who told him that her husband had some urgent business that would prevent him from meeting Mr. Lerner at the agreed-upon time. After Mr. Lerner told her not to worry, she politely repeated

Mooshiwake gozaimasen. (I am very sorry.)

Mr. Lerner thought "Like husband, like wife," but one thing that bothered him was that her *gozaimasen* sounded like *gozaasen*.

*　　　*　　　*

Some consonants are pronounced softly in rapid speech, especially in the middle of a word. The *m* sound is one of them. Even in careful speech, the *m* sound in Japanese is softer than the "m" in English; the lips are not pressed against each other strongly with the Japanese *m*. Some people, usually women, pronounce this sound with the lips never touching; consequently

Sumimasen (I am sorry) sounds like
Suimasen, and sometimes *Suiasen.*
すいません　　　　　　　すいあせん
gozaimasu sounds like *gozaiasu,* ございあす
gozaimasen like *gozaiasen* or *gozaasen.*
ございあせん
ござあせん

Another soft consonant is the *w* sound. In careful speech, too, the lips are not rounded as much as with the English "w" sound, and in rapid speech it is pronounced even more softly. Therefore *kawaii* (cute, lovely) sounds like *kaaii,*

114

and *kawarimashita* (it changed) like *kaarimashita*.

The nasalized *g* sound is also pronounced very softly by some people. This is a sound like the "ng" sound in "sing." When this *g* sound is pronounced softly, *gi* sounds like *ni*; consequently *kagi* (key) and *kani* (crab) sound similar. Sometimes the nasalized *ga* sounds like *a*; therefore *magatte-kudasai* (Please turn) sounds like

maatte-kudasai
which is very close to
mawatte-kudasai. (Please go around.)

In this case the soft pronunciation of the *w* sound is also involved. Likewise, *sagatte-kudasai* (Please go back) sounds like

Saatte-kudasai.
which is very close to
Sawatte-kudasai. (Please touch it.)

Sounds difficult to hear
(3) voiceless vowels

Mr. Lerner can now express almost anything he wants to say in Japanese, but he still has difficulty in distinguishing two similar-sounding words. Just yesterday, when talking about a musical show on TV, Miss Yoshida said

Shikaisha-ga amari yoku nakatta-desu-ne.
(The master of ceremonies wasn't very good.)

But he couldn't understand because he thought she had said

Kaisha-ga amari yoku nakatta-desu-ne.
(The company wasn't very good.)

* * *

In standard Japanese the *i* and *u* sounds tend to become voiceless in certain circumstances; a devocalized vowel sounds as if it were whispered, and is hard to hear. In the case of *shikaisha,* the *i* sound in *shi* is often devocalized, and the word sounds like

sh-kaisha,

The most common case where a vowel becomes voiceless is at the end of a sentence; the *u* sound in *desu* and *masu* in such sentences as

Soo-desu. (That's right.)　そうで<u>す</u>。
Ikimasu. (I'm going.)　　行きま<u>す</u>。

is very often devocalized. However, when the sentence is said with a rising intonation as a question, the *u* sound in *desu* or *masu* is not devocalized.

116

Namely, the *u* sound of

>   *Ikimasu?* (Are you going?)

is not devocalized.

Also when the *i* and *u* sounds fall between voiceless consonants, as in the following words, the middle vowels are often devocalized.

shika (only)	しか
tsuki (moon)	つき
kikai (machine)	きかい

And the *i* and *u* sounds at the beginning of a word are often devocalized when followed by a voiceless consonant and if the accent does not fall on the following syllable, as in

ikimashita	いきました
utatte-kudasai	うたってください

Therefore *ikimashita* (I went) can sound like *kimashita* (I came) and *utatte-kudasai* (please sing) like *tatte-kudasai* (please stand). To distinguish the two, one should carefully listen to the first syllable.

Answering with phrases

Mr. Mori, the director of the company, asked Mr. Lerner when his project would be completed, and he answered

Raigetsu-no tooka-goro-ni.
(On about the 10th of next month.)

Miss Yoshida, who was there with them, later told him that answering a superior with a phrase sounds rude. He wondered why he had to use a complete sentence when the Japanese leave out the last part of their sentences so often.

*　　　*　　　*

When answering questions requiring factual information such as dates, times, names and figures, one should use verbs in polite speech. For instance, when someone has asked you what time you came, it is rude to say

Sanji-ni. (At 3 o'clock.)
unless he is a close friend. One should say

Sanji-ni kimashita. (I came at 3 o'clock.)

instead. When answering what time it is, you should add *desu* as in

Sanji-desu.

instead of saying *Sanji*.

In Mr. Lerner's case above, he should have said something like

Raigetsu-no tooka-goro-ni dekimasu.

来月の　十日ごろに　できます。

(It will be completed around the 10th of next
month.)

Raigetsu-no tooka-goro-ni naru-to omoimasu.

(I think it will be about the 10th of next month.)

Sometimes answering with a phrase can be appropriate. One case is when the tone indicates that
a verb phrase is understood although not stated, as
in

Raigetsu-no tooka-goro-niwa. . .
来月の　十日ごろには……

(*dekimasu* is left out)

In this case, a dangling tone must be used instead
of a falling tone which sounds definite.

Another case is when using polite expressions
such as

Nochi-hodo (Later — more polite than *Ato-de.*)
Gotsugoo-no yoroshii toki-ni (Whenever it suits
you.)

Also, when preceded by such polite expressions as
Hai., Soo-desu-ne. . . or *mooshiwake arimasen-ga,*
answering with a phrase can be polite.

A: *Ikura-gurai kakarimasu-ka.*

(How much will it cost?)

B: *Hai. Chotto otakaku narimashite mooshiwake
arimasen-ga, ichiman-en-hodo.*

(Well, I'm sorry it is a little expensive . . .
about ¥10,000.)

The use of . . .*nante* (to do. . .)

Mr. Lerner and Miss Yoshida went to a restaurant last Saturday evening. The restaurant was unusually crowded and they were told that they would have to wait for half an hour. Mr. Lerner said

Nagaku matsu-nowa iya-desu-ne.
(We don't want to wait for a long time, do we?)

and Miss Yoshida agreed saying

Ee. Bakarashii-desu-ne, sanjippun-mo matsu-nante.
(No. It's absurd to wait for 30 minutes.)

Mr. Lerner realized that he had not used . . .*nante* in this way; he had always used it after nouns, as in *tabako-nante kirai-desu.* (I don't like smoking.)

*　　　*　　　*

. . .*nante* is used as a contraction of *nado* or *nado-to yuu mono/koto/no*, as in

Tanaka-san-nante. . .
(*Tanaka-san-nado* — such a person as Tanaka-san)

osake-nante. . .　お酒なんて……
(*osake-nado-to yuu mono* — such a thing as alcohol)

Sometimes a verb phrase can precede *nante*, which is used as a contraction of *nado-to yuu koto/no*, as in

asa hayaku okiru-nante . . .
朝　早く　起きるなんて……

120

(*asa hayaku okiru-nado-to yuu koto* — such a thing as getting up early)

anna hito-to tsukiau-nante . . .

(*anna hito-to tsukiau-nado-to yuu-no* — such a thing as associating with a person like him)

Using *nante* in this way usually implies dislike, contempt, surprise, admiration, etc. As compared with "(verb)-*nowa*" in *matsu-nowa* and *hataraku-nowa*, *matsu-nante* and *hataraku-nante* express stronger emotion. For instance, *nichiyoobi-ni-made hataraku-nowa* (working even on Sundays) is usually followed by such statements as

. . . *kanshin-shimasen.* (I don't think it good.)
. . . *yarisugi-desu.* (is going too far.)

On the other hand, *nichiyoobi-ni made hataraku-nante* is usually followed by an emotional statement such as

. . . *watashi-wa iya-desu-ne.* (I wouldn't do that.)
erai mon-desu-ne. (is really great, isn't it?)

The use of . . . *wake-desu*
(the situation is . . .)

Yesterday afternoon a Mrs. Watanabe came to see Mr. Lerner at the office. She explained that she had been looking for a foreigner to write about his or her experiences working with Japanese for the magazine she works for and that a friend had recently told her about Mr. Lerner. After this explanation she said

Sore-de onegai-ni agatta wake-desu-ga.
それで　お願いに　あがつた　わけです。
(So I came to ask this favor.)

Mr. Lerner realized that he was not yet able to use *wake* in this way; he would have said something like *Dakara onegai-ni kimashita* instead.

*　　*　　*

Wake is used in various ways. One usage is in referring to "reason" or "cause" as in *Wake-wa shirimasen-ga* (I don't know why). Another is the usage referring to "situation" as in Mrs. Watanabe's case above. Her sentence literally means "The situation is that I came to ask your favor in the circumstances I have just explained." When one wants to conclude an explanation one often uses *wake* as in

Soo yuu wake-desu.
そう　いう　わけです。
(That's how it is.)

. . . to yuu wake-desu.
(The situation is . . .)

In other words, . . . *wake-desu* is used to show that

one feels one has explained the situation with the right procedure. It is used when one has completed a portion of what one has to say; it is something like a paragraph-ending mark in spoken language.

It is thus not appropriate to use ... *wake-desu* before one has fully completed what one has to explain. For instance, saying something like

Kinoo Nikkoo-e itta wake-desu.
(I went to Nikko yesterday.)
Watashi-wa kaisha-o yameta wake-desu.
(I quit the job.)

is not appropriate for starting a conversation.

Male speech used toward women

At lunch time yesterday Mr. Takada said to Mr. Lerner and several other male colleagues

Meshi, kui-ni ikoo-ka.
めし、食いに　行こうか。
(Shall we go eat lunch? — male speech)

As they were about to leave, Miss Yoshida and another woman came by. Then Mr. Takada asked them to join them, saying

Ohiru, tabe-ni ikanai?
おひる、食べに　行かない？
(How about going out for lunch?)

Mr. Lerner was interested in the change in Mr. Takada's speech; he wondered if men change their speech depending on whether they are talking to men or women.

*　　　*　　　*

Some words are considered to be used mainly by men and some by women, but the distinction is not fixed. Generally speaking, men talk very much like men between themselves but when they talk to women they tend to modify their speech so that it becomes similar to women's speech. For instance, the word *meshi* (meal, cooked rice) is usually used by men when talking with men of equal status. When asking a superior to go out for lunch a man would say something like

Shokuji-ni nasaimasen-ka.
(Would you like to go eat?)
Chuushoku-ni irasshaimasen-ka.

(Won't you go out for lunch?)

When men talk to women, they tend to adopt the women's term, *ohiru*.

Women usually use women's terms among themselves; a woman would invite her colleague to lunch saying something like *Ohiru-ni ikanai?* or *Ohiru-gohan-ni irassharanai?* (*Ohiru-gohan* is even more feminine than *ohiru*.) Women do not usually adopt men's speech when talking to men. They wouldn't say something like *Meshi, kui-ni ikimashoo* to men. Women change their speech, however, when talking to children; both men and women often adopt children's terms when talking with children.

In a similar way, an expression like . . . *kashira* (I wonder) undergoes a change depending on whom one talks to; men do not use . . . *kashira* with other men but they sometimes use it when talking to women, especially to younger women.

Expressions meaning 'must'

When Mr. Takada complained about a headache yesterday afternoon, Miss Yoshida attributed it to his excessive drinking, and said

Osake-o herasanakucha dame-desu-yo.
(*lit.* If you don't decrease your drinking, it won't do.)

Mr. Lerner realized that this expression ... *nakucha dame-desu* corresponds to the English "one must ..." or "one has to ..." just as ... *nakereba narimasen* does, and wondered if there are other such expressions.

*　　*　　*

The most common way to indicate that one must, or has to, do something is to combine two phrases, one each from two groups, as indicated below.

1.　phrases meaning "if one doesn't ..."
　... *nakereba* contracted into ... *nakerya* or ... *nakya* ……なければ、……なけりゃ、……なきゃ
　... *nakute-wa* contracted into ... *nakucha*
2　phrases meaning "it won't do"
　narimasen なりません
　ikemasen いけません
　dame-desu だめです

All these phrases can be combined freely as long as the phrase from (1) comes first. For instance, ... *nakereba* can be followed by any of the three listed in (2); namely ... *nakereba narimasen*, ... *nakereba ikemasen* and ... *nakereba dame-desu* are all used.

In all of these combinations, the phrases in (2) can be left out without causing difficulty in understanding, as in

Osake-o herasanakucha . . . (You should drink less.)
Moo kaeranakya . . . (I have to go home now.)

Among the three expressions in (2), *narimasen* sounds more formal than the others, and *dame-desu* the most familiar. *Ikemasen* and *Dame-desu* can be used alone, as in

Child: *Kore, ima tabete-mo ii?*
        (May I eat it now?)
Mother: *Iie, ikemasen. Gohan-no ato-ni shinasai.*
        (No, you may not. Eat it after the
        meal.)

Patient: *Osake-wa doo-deshoo? Nonde-mo
         kamaimasen-ka.*
         (What about alcohol? Is it all right to
         have some?)
Doctor: *Dame-desu. Toobun nomanaide-kudasai.*
         (No. You shouldn't drink for the time
         being.)

Narimasen is not used in this way in conversation.

'You' in Japanese

On Monday mornings Mr. Lerner's colleagues usually ask each other if they went somewhere over the weekend. Mr. Lerner once answered

Ginza-e ikimashita. Anata-wa?
(I went to Ginza. How about you?)

and was told by Miss Yoshida to use the other person's name instead of *anata* as in

Ginza-e ikimashita. Tanaka-san-wa?
銀座へ　行きました。田中さんは？

He now tries not to use *anata* unnecessarily, but still wonders how he should refer to someone he does not know in the second person.

*　　　*　　　*

Words corresponding to the English "you," as well as those corresponding to "I," are left out whenever possible. For instance, when asking

Kinoo-wa dokoka-e ikimashita-ka.
(Did you go somewhere yesterday?)

no word meaning "you" is used because it is obvious. If you said

Anata-wa kinoo dokoka-e ikimashita-ka.

it would mean "Did YOU go somewhere yesterday?" in contrast with others.

Polite expressions also serve to make communication possible without the use of a word meaning "you." When telling a stranger that he has dropped something on the street, you will say

> *Anoo, nanika otosaremashita-yo.*
> (Excuse me. You dropped something.)

Otosareru is a polite expression referring to someone other than the speaker, so *anata* is not
necessary. Or, more often, one says

> *Anoo, nanika ochimashita-yo.*
> あのう、なにか　おちましたよ。
> (*lit.* Excuse me; something has been dropped.)

using a sentence which does not require a word
meaning "you."

But sometimes a word meaning "you" is
necessary as in asking "How about you?" In such
cases, the name of the other person plus a term of
respect is used as in *Tanaka-san-wa?* or *Michiko-san-
wa?*

Titles are also used; those worthy of respect
are often preferred to personal names, such as
shachoo (company director), *sensee* (professor,
doctor), *daijin* (government minister), etc. Terms
indicating family relations are also used — *okusan*
(your wife, someone's wife), *otoosan* (your father,
someone's father), etc. Sometimes one's situation
can be used as in

> *Kore, okyakusan-no-ja arimasen-ka.*
> これ、お客さんのじゃ　ありませんか。
> (Isn't this yours? — said to a customer by a
storekeeper.)

Expressions accompanying an action

Mr. Lerner and a couple of colleagues went driving in the country in Mr. Takada's car last Saturday. They had a good time, but on their way home one of the front wheels got caught in a pothole, and they had to push the car up. The men raised the car together, saying

Se-e-no!
せえの！

Mr. Lerner was interested in this type of expression and wondered what other exclamations are used when starting an action.

*   *   *

There are several expressions, called *kakegoe,* used when one starts an action that requires some physical effort. *Seeno* is used when two or more people start some strenuous action together. With the sound *See* they get ready and with *no!* they start exerting their strength together.

Ichi-ni-no san!
一二の三！
(One, two and three!)

is also used to start a group action. In this case too, people get ready with *Ichi-ni-no,* and start the action with *san!* These two expressions are also used when starting a song or some other musical performance.

When one gathers one's own physical strength to do something, one says

Yoisho!

よいしょ！

This is most often used when raising, pulling, pushing or carrying heavy objects. It is also used when one stretches to reach an object on a high shelf or the like.

Dokkoisho is used when one pulls oneself together to start an action. Elderly people tend to use it often when starting various actions such as standing up from a seat, climbing steps, bending down to pick something up, and even sitting down.

Wasshoi!

is used when carrying an *omikoshi,* a portable shrine, at a festival. It is usually repeated as in

Wasshoi, wasshoi.
わっしょい、わっしょい。

when people carry the *omikoshi* along the street.

The polite expression of opposition

Mr. Lerner and Mr. Takada handed a short description of a plan they had been working on to Mr. Mori, the director of the company. Mr. Mori glanced through it and suggested a change. The suggestion concerned the point that they had worked the hardest on, so they had to oppose it, but Mr. Lerner was not sure if he could do so politely. Then Mr. Takada said, after a slight pause,

Soo-deshoo-ka.
そうでしょうか。
(I wonder.)

Then Mr. Mori seemed to think again, and started to modify his suggestion.

* * *

To express one's opposition politely, one avoids using such direct expressions as *Iie, chigaimasu* (No, you're wrong), *Sonna koto-wa arimasen* (There's no such thing), or *Watashi-wa soo omoimasen* (I don't think that way).

One way to make the expression more reserved is to change the end of the sentence by using such indirect expressions as . . . *n-ja nai-deshoo-ka* (I'm afraid it is. . .), . . . *ja nai-ka-to omoimasu* (I'm afraid it might be. . .) or . . . *yoo-desu-ga* (it seems. . .), as in

Chotto chigau-n-ja nai-deshoo-ka.
ちょっと　ちがうんじゃ　ないでしょうか。
(I'm afraid it is somewhat incorrect.)
Doomo soo-ja nai yoo-desu-ga.
どうも　そうじゃ　ない　ようですが。
(Somehow it does not seem that way to me.)

Together with reserved endings, such adverbs as *chotto* (a little) or *doomo* (somehow) are often used, and sometimes the rest of the sentence is left out after them, as in

>*Sore-wa chotto. . .*
>(That seems to be wrong/inconvenient, etc.)
>*Doomo sono ten-wa. . .*
>(On that point I can hardly agree, etc.)

Another way to suggest that you do not agree and want the other person to reconsider is to say

>*Soo-deshoo-ka.*
>(*lit.* Is that so, I wonder?)

When using this to imply opposition the tone is important. It should be said with a dangling tone instead of a definite one so that you can show you are not certain. And it must be said after a slight lapse of time; silence serves to show that you are hesitating before voicing your opposition. If you sound very ready to oppose, no polite expression can express reserve.

'O' plus stem plus *desu-ka*

When leaving the office the other day Mr. Lerner met an elderly man in the hall. The man works for a company in the same building and is one of Mr. Lerner's nodding acquaintances. He said

Okaeri-desu-ka.
お帰りですか。
(*lit.* Is it your going home?)

Mr. Lerner answered *Hai,* and added *Shitsuree-shimasu* (Good-bye — *lit.* Excuse me). While doing so, he wondered what difference there is between *Okaeri-desu-ka* and *Okaeri-ni narimasu-ka,* both of which mean "Are you going home?"

* * *

O or *go,* polite prefixes, plus the stem (the first part of the *masu*-form) of verbs and *desu-ka* makes a polite question. *Okaeri-desu-ka* is formed from the verb *kaeru* (to go home), and *Gobenkyoo-desu-ka* is from the verb *benkyoo-suru.*

Both "*O*-plus-the stem-plus-*ni narimasu-ka*" and "*O*-plus-the stem-plus-*desu-ka*" are polite questions. The difference is that "*O*-plus-the stem-plus-*desu-ka*" sounds less direct and more refined or reserved. For instance,

Nanji-ni okaeri-ni narimasu-ka.
(What time is he/are you coming back?)
and
Nanji-ni okaeri-desu-ka.

mean the same thing, but the latter sounds more refined, less demanding, and polite.

Because this form sounds more reserved, it is often used in social situations. When a guest is leaving, for instance, the host(ess) will often say

Moo okaeri-desu-ka.
もう　お帰りですか。
(Are you leaving so soon?)
to show regret over the guest's being unable to stay longer.

Sometimes this type of question is used to show one's concern rather than to seek factual information. Saying *Okaeri-desu-ka* in the case of Mr. Lerner's acquaintance can be paraphrased as "I see you are going home. Good-bye." In the same way

Odekake-desu-ka.
おでかけですか。
(*lit.* Is it your going out?)

said as a greeting usually means "I see you're going out. Have a good time."

135

The noun plus *desu* form

While taking a walk last Saturday afternoon Mr. Lerner happened to pass near Mr. Okada's apartment, and dropped by. The door was closed and nobody answered. When he was about to leave, a neighbor, an elderly woman, came out and said

> *Okada-san, go-ryokoo-no yoo-desu-yo.*
> (It seems the Okadas are traveling.)

Mr. Lerner thought he would have said

> *Okada-san, ryokoo-shite-irassharu yoo-desu-yo.*

to mean the same thing, and wondered if the neighbor's expression was more appropriate.

* * *

When the verb is obvious and can be understood without mentioning it, it is often left out and just the preceding noun is used. For instance, one will often say things like the following when asked about one's family members.

> *Ima ofuro-desu.* (He's taking a bath.)
> いま　おふろです。
> *Ima sentaku-desu.* (She's doing the laundry.)
> *Benkyoo-desu.* (She's studying.)
> 勉強です。
> *Kaimono-desu.* (She went shopping.)
> 買い物です。

Such verbs as *suru* (to do), *iku,* (to go) and *hairu* (to enter, to take a bath) are often left out. Using verbs in such cases sounds wordy, although not incorrect.

136

Especially kanji compound nouns are often used without *suru* or *iku,* as in

> *Kyoo-wa kaigi-da-shi, ashita-kara shutchoo-da-kara, uchi-ni iru hima-ga nai.*
> (I'll be attending a meeting today and going on a business trip tomorrow; I won't be home for a while.)

To describe what happened in the past, *deshita* or *datta* is used as in

> *Kyoo-wa PTA-datta-node, rusu-deshita.*
> (I went out to attend a PTA meeting, and wasn't home today.)
> *Kyonen-wa kodomo-ga juken-deshita-kara taihen-deshita.*
> (My child took his entrance exam last year and I had to do much for him.)

When choosing a meal at a restaurant, a noun plus *desu* is very often used as in

> *Boku-wa sashimi-da-kedo, kimi-wa?*
> ぼくは　さしみだけど、君は？
> (I'll take the *sashimi*; what about you?)

Shikata-ga arimasen

Mrs. Matsumoto, one of Mr. Lerner's colleagues came late again yesterday morning and Miss Yoshida had to do part of her work for her. When someone said something critical of Mrs. Matsumoto for frequently being late, Miss Yoshida said

Akachan-ga iru-n-desu-kara, shikata-ga arimasen.
(Since she has a baby, it can't be helped.)

to defend her. Mr. Lerner was interested in this use of *shikata-ga nai* and wondered if it was common.

* * *

The word *shikata* by itself means "how to do, way of doing" and *shikata-ga nai* means "there is no way to handle the situation." Thus it is often used to express resignation, as in

WIFE: *Moo saishuu-no basu-ga dete-shimatta-wa.*
(The last bus has already left.)
HUSBAND: *Shikata-ga nai. Takushii-ni noroo.*
しかたが ない。タクシーに 乗ろう。
(It can't be helped. Let's take a taxi.)

Sometimes . . .*yori shikata-ga nai* is used to indicate that there is no other way, as in

Takushii-ni noru-yori shikata-ga nai.
(There is no other way but to take a taxi.)
Otoshita mono-wa akirameru-yori shikata-ga nai.
(What is lost is lost. There is nothing we can do but to give up.)

As in Miss Yoshida's speech, this expression is also used to express the speaker's leniency, as in

Kodomo-da-kara shikata-ga arimasen.
子どもだから　しかたが　ありません。
(Since he is only a child, he can be excused — for doing such a thing.)

Sometimes *...nomo shikata-ga nai* is used to mean "it is understandable and can be excused" or "one should not criticize someone for . . .ing), as in

Akanboo-ga iru-n-da-kara, okureru-nomo shikata-ga nai.
(Since she has a baby, it is excusable that she comes late.)

Gekkyuu-ga yasui-n-da-kara, amari hatarakanai-nomo shikata-ga nai-deshoo.
(Since they are not paid well, we cannot expect them to work enthusiastically.)

The various uses of *yoku*

When Mr. Lerner and his colleagues were talking about music at lunch time yesterday, Mr. Kato said that he had been practicing singing and would like them to hear him sing some time. After he left, everybody talked about his being a poor singer, and one of them said

> *Yoku anna koto-ga ieru-ne.*
> (*lit.* He can say such a thing well.)

Mr. Lerner understood that they were critical of Mr. Kato boasting about his singing, but was not sure about using *yoku* in this way.

* * *

The word *yoku* is commonly used in daily conversation in various meanings. One is its use in the sense of ''well,'' ''skillfully'' or ''thoroughly.''

> *Yoku kangaete-kara henji-shimasu.*
> よく 考えてから 返事します。
> (I will answer after giving good thought to it.)
> *Amari yoku hanasemasen.*
> (I can't speak very well.)
> *Ano-hito, yoku hatarakimasu-ne.*
> (He works hard, doesn't he?)
> *Yoku irasshaimashita.*
> (I'm glad you could come — *lit.* You came in a good way.)

Another use is to refer to quantity or frequency, meaning ''a lot'' or ''often'' as in

> *Kinoo-wa yoku furimashita-ne.*
> きのうは よく ふりましたね。

140

(It rained a lot yesterday.)
Wakai koro-wa yoku eega-o mimashita.
(I often saw movies when I was young.)

The third use is as an expression of sarcasm, corresponding to the English "how can he. . .?" or "he dares. . . ," as used by Mr. Lerner's colleague above.

Yoku anna bakana koto-ga dekiru-ne.
よく あんな ばかな ことが できるね。
(How can he do such an absurd thing?)
Kimi, yoku(mo) sonna koto-ga boku-ni taishite ieru-na.
(What nerve you have to say such a thing to me!)

These three common uses can be distinguished from the context, not from the form of the sentence. For instance, the following sentence can mean three different things depending on the situation.

Yoku kimashita-ne.
1. I'm glad you came.
2. He used to come here very often, didn't he?
3. How dare he be here to see us?

Aizuchi-bijin ('Response Beauty')

Mr. Lerner likes to watch TV programs reporting on current affairs. A few days ago when watching one of these programs, he noticed that a woman speaker said nothing but *aizuchi,* as in

MAN: *Kondo-no jiken-desu-keredo* . . . (Concerning what happened this time. . .)
WOMAN: *Ee.*
MAN: *Sono gen'in-wa iroiro aru-towa omoimasu-ga* . . . (I think there is more than one cause behind it, but. . .)
WOMAN: *Ee.*

　こんどの　事件ですけれど……
　ええ。
　その　原因は　いろいろ　あるとは　思いますが…
　ええ。

In this way the man talked on and on and the woman just gracefully gave *aizuchi* and said nothing to express her own views. After that Mr. Lerner paid particular attention to this whenever he watched TV and found that this a rather common pattern.

＊　　　＊　　　＊

In a Japanese conversation the listener gives frequent *aizuchi* — reply words such as *hai, ee,* and *soo-desu-ka* — to show that he has been listening attentively and has understood so far, and to encourage the speaker to go on. *Aizuchi* are essential in a conversation between two persons.

The Japanese notion of what a conversation should be is of a flow of speech made by two people. Rather than one person continuing to talk and the other person listening quietly, Japanese speakers like to have the listener positively participate in the conversation by giving *aizuchi* and sometimes even finishing up the speaker's sentences. Thus, it requires two people, a speaker and a listener giving *aizuchi,* to make Japanese speech natural.

Even in the case of TV or radio programs, people often find it easier to talk to someone giving appropriate *aizuchi* than to talk to the microphone alone. Especially in "how-to" programs such as those on cooking, flower arrangement, gardening, etc., a good *aizuchi*-giver with whom the audience can identify itself is indispensable.

These *aizuchi-bijins, aizuchi*-giving beautiful young women, thus play an essential role in making the program sound natural.

Kaeroo-tto
(I guess I'll be going home now)

Last night Mr. Lerner and Mr. Takada stayed late at the office working. When the work was finished and they were getting ready to leave, Mr. Takada said

>*Sorosoro kaeroo-tto.*
>そろそろ　帰ろうっと。

(Shall I be going home now? — *lit.* I'm leaving slowly.)

Mr. Lerner remembered that the Japanese often talk to themselves in this way, and wondered what the last part *tto* means.

*　　　*　　　*

People sometimes talk to themselves when about to start an action. For instance, they say something like

>*Saa, neyoo-ka.* (Well, shall I go to bed?)
>*Moo okiru-to suru-kana.* (Shall I get up now?)

They also use sentences with *tto* preceded by the volitional form, namely . . . *oo* or . . *yoo* as in *ikoo* or *okiyoo*. The last *tto* is from . . . *to omou* (I think). This *to* is usually preceded by the stop *t* in this usage; therefore *kaeroo-to omou* becomes *kaeroo-tto*.

Mr. Lerner could have said

>*Sorosoro kaeroo-ka(na).*
>そろそろ　帰ろうか（な）。

too. The difference between . . . *ka(na)* and . . . *tto* is that the latter sounds more familiar and is often used by children. When an adult chooses *kaeroo-tto,* it has the effect of sounding a little humorous.

When going home in the evening after playing with their friends, many Japanese children used to say in a singing tone

Kaeru-ga naku-kara kaeroo-tto.
(*lit.* Since frogs are croaking, I will go home.)

Here a pun between *kaeru* (go home) and *kaeru* (a frog) is used. These two words are pronounced in similar ways, although the accent is different (to mean "going home," *ka* is pronounced higher than *-eru,* while *ka* is pronounced lower when *kaeru* means frog). Incidentally, NTT uses a large artificial frog in their current commercial on TV urging people to call their family and tell them when they are coming home — namely, to make *kaeru-kooru* (going-home telephone calls).

...ta tokoro & ...ta bakari

When Mr. Okada came to Mr. Lerner's office yesterday afternoon to discuss business, Miss Yoshida asked him if he would like some tea and cake, but Mr. Okada said

Ie, ima shokuji-shite-kita bakari-desu-kara.
(No, thank you. I have just had lunch.)

Miss Yoshida looked disappointed and said,

Soo-desu-ka. Ima keeki-o kitta tokoro-desu-noni.
(Oh, is that right? I have just cut a cake.)

Mr. Lerner wondered what difference there is between ...*ta tokoro* and ...*ta bakari*.

*   *   *

Both the past form plus *tokoro* and the past form plus *bakari* indicate that an action has just been completed, as in

Nihon-ni tsuita tokoro-desu.
(I have just arrived in Japan.)
Nihon-ni tsuita bakari-desu.
(I have just arrived in Japan.)

But their implications are different. When one uses ...*ta tokoro* it emphasizes that the action has just been completed, as in

Gohan-ga taketa tokoro-desu.
ごはんが　たけた　ところです。
(The rice is cooked.)

which can imply such things as that the speaker

146

has finished such tasks or that the rice is warm and good to eat. When Miss Yoshida said *keeki-o kitta tokoro-desu,* she implied that she wanted Mr. Okada to have some good cake.

On the other hand, . . .*ta bakari* implies that an action has been completed but the following due development has not started yet, as in

> *Ima okita bakari-desu.*
> いま　おきた　ばかりです。
> (I have just got up.)

which implies that the speaker has not yet done what is expected after getting up, such as dressing or having breakfast. Thus, one may say things like

> *Ima okita bakari-de shokuyoku-ga nai.*
> (I have just got up and don't have any appetite.)
> *Ima okita bakari-desu-kara, mada dekakeraremasen.*
> (I have just got up now; I can't leave home yet.)

When Mr. Okada said *shokuji-shite-kita bakari-desu,* he implied that his stomach was still full and he was not yet ready for tea and cake.

Jibun (One's self)

Yesterday afternoon when Mr. Lerner and Miss Yoshida were talking during their coffee break, Mr. Mori, the director of the company, came over with an envelope with red and white strings on it. It contained some money as a gift for someone's wedding, and Mr. Mori asked Miss Yoshida to write his name on it for him because she was a good calligrapher. She said yes but added

Demo, hontoo-wa gojibun-de okaki-ni natta hoo-ga. . .
(It might be better for you to write it yourself.)

Mr. Lerner was interested in the use of the word *go-jibun* and realized that he had never used it himself.

*   *   *

The word *jibun* means "one's self," and is used to refer to anyone, as in

Jibun-de kakimashita.
自分で　書きました。
(I wrote it myself.)
Ima sunde-iru uchi-wa jibun-no uchi-da soo-desu.
(He says that he lives in his own house.)
Sore-wa jibun-ga warui-n-dayo.
それは　自分が　わるいんだよ。
(That's your own fault.)

To make the expression more polite, one adds *go* as Miss Yoshida did. One uses this as in

Gojibun-de oide-ni naranakute-mo kekkoo-desu.
(You don't have to go yourself.)

Jibun was once used to mean "I" in the military forces; they had to decide on one term to mean "I" because there were many terms used to refer to the speaker himself. In present usage, however, *jibun* is not usually used to mean "I."

Jibun-de means "for yourself," "using one's own capacity"; to mean "by oneself" as in "I live alone," *hitori-de* is used instead of *jibun-de*. It is wrong to say *Jibun-de sunde-imasu*; instead one should say

> *Hitori-de kurashite-imasu.*
> ひとりで　くらしています。
> (I live alone.)

人は、人、自分は　自分。

The word used in contrast with *jibun* is *hito* (others), as in

> *Hito-wa hito, jibun-wa jibun.*

(One should go one's own way — *lit*. Others are others; oneself is oneself.)

> *Hito-no koto-yori, jibun-no koto-o kangaenasai.*

(Rather than bothering about others, think of yourself.)

The second sentence is used in a case such as someone advising you to do something like quitting smoking or getting married regardless of his own condition.

Uses of *koso*

Yesterday afternoon at work, Mr. Lerner almost ran into a woman when turning a corner. He stopped short and was about to apologize, when the woman said

    Shitsuree-shimashita. (Excuse me.)

So he wanted to say

    "Oh, excuse ME."

because he thought he was the one to blame, but he could not think of an appropriate expression and just said *Sumimasen* (I'm sorry.)

    *   *   *

When someone has apologized or thanked you and you want to say that it is you who should say so, *koso* is used as in

    Kochira-koso.
    こちらこそ。
    (*lit.* It's my side.)

. . . *koso* is added to the word or phrase you want to emphasize as in

    Ashita-koso hayaku okiyoo.
    あしたこそ　早く　おきよう。
    (I will certainly get up early TOMORROW.)
    Kore-koso, gendai-no kiseki-desu.
    (THIS is the miracle of this age.)

Kochira-koso is used frequently when responding to expressions of gratitude or apology as in

I. A. *Iroiro arigatoo-gozaimashita.*
(Thank you very much. You've been so kind.)

B. *Iie, kochira-koso, taihen osewa-ni narimashita.*
(No, it's me that should thank you for your kindness.)

II. A. *Gobusata-itashimashita.*
(I'm sorry I didn't write to you sooner.)

B. *Iie, kochira-koso, taihen gobusata-itashimashita.*
(No, I should apologize for not writing to you.)

Expressions of consideration are also followed by . . . *koso*, as in

III. A. *Otsukaresama-deshita.*
おつかれさまでした。
(Thank you. You must be tired now.)

B. *Iie, sensee-koso otsukare-deshoo.*
いいえ、先生こそ　おつかれでしょう。
(No, YOU must be tired after doing so much for me.)

In all of the examples above, *Kochira-koso* can be used alone, leaving the rest unsaid.

Sometimes . . . *koso* is used in responding to compliments, as in

IV. A. *Maa, kyoo-wa totemo suteki-ne.*
(You look very nice today.)

B. *Ara, Yoshiko-san-koso!*
(Oh, YOU look gorgeous.)

The last conversation is between female friends.

Phrases with *ne*

Mr. Lerner happened to pass by Miss Yoshida when she was talking on the phone yesterday afternoon, and heard her say

Warui-kedo-ne, ashita-wa-ne, tsugoo-ga tsukanai-n-de-ne, asatte-ni shite-kurenai?
(Sorry, but I cannot make it tomorrow; could you make it the day after tomorrow instead?)

Mr. Lerner was interested in her frequent use of *ne* which was added to almost every phrase she used. He wondered how often *ne* can be used within one sentence.

* * *

The particle *ne* is added when the speaker wants the listener to agree or feel the same way. It is often used at the end of a sentence both in polite and familiar speech.

Ii otenki-desu-ne. (Fine day, isn't it? — polite)
Ii tenki-da-ne. (Fine day, isn't it? — familiar)
Ashita oide-kudasaimasu-ne.
(You will come tomorrow, won't you? — polite)
Ashita kite-kureru-ne.
(Now you will come tomorrow, won't you? — familiar)

However, adding *ne* to a phrase within a sentence can be done only in familiar speech.

Ashita-ne, kite-kureru-ne.
Ha-ga itakute-ne, ikenai-n-da.
(I have a toothache so I can't come.)

152

Sometimes more than one phrase in a sentence is followed by *ne*, as in

> *Doomo-ne, ha-ga itakute-ne, ikenai-n-da.*
> どうもね、歯が いたくてね、行けないんだ。
> (**My tooth really aches and I can't come.**)

In fact, *ne* can be added to any phrase; it can be added not only to nouns and adverbs but also to particles such as *wa, ga, de, no, e, ni* and *o*.

> *Kore-o-ne, Yamada-san-no-ne, tsukue-no ue-ni-ne, oite-kurenai?*
> これをね、山田さんのね、机の 上にね、おいてくれない？
> (**Please put this on Mr. Yamada's desk, would you?**)

The frequency of *ne* is proportional to the degree of familiarity; adding it to many phrases makes the speech very familiar. And it sometimes indicates the speaker's eagerness to make sure that the listener has understood.

... *no koto-desu* meaning
'I'm referring to . . . '

When Mr. Lerner and Miss Yoshida were talking at lunch time yesterday, Mr. Takada came over
and asked

Are, doo natta? (What happened to that?)

Mr. Lerner did not know what Mr. Takada was
referrring to, so he was going to ask *Nan-desu-ka*
(What is it?), when Miss Yoshida said

Nan-no koto-desu-ka. (What are you referring
to?)

Mr. Lerner realized that he was not yet able to use
... *no koto* in this kind of situation.

* * *

The appropriate expression for asking what the
other person is referring to is *Nan-no koto-desu-ka.*
Saying *Nan-desu-ka* or *Nani-o itte-imasu-ka* (*lit.*
What are you saying?) can be understood, but
these expressions can sound as if you are
reprimanding the other.

... *no koto* means "about . . . ," as in

Ashita-no kaigi-no koto-desu-ga. . .
あしたの　会議の　ことですが……
(It's about tomorrow's conference.)
Yosan-no koto-de gosoodan-ga arimasu.
(I'd like to discuss the budget with you.)

... *ni tsuite* (concerning. . .) will be
understood, as in

Ashita-no kaigi-ni tsuite-desu-ga. . .

154

Yosan-ni tsuite gosoodan-ga arimasu.

but . . . *no koto* sounds more conversational.

Besides these usages, . . . *no koto* is used with such verbs as *kangaeru* (think), *hanasu* (talk) or *shinpai-suru* (worry), as in

Shiken-no koto-o kangaeru-to shinpai-de shoo-ga nai.
(When I think about the exam, I am very much worried.)
Ima, kimi-no koto-o hanashite-ita-n-da-yo.
いま、君の ことを 話していたんだよ。
(We were just talking about you.)

INDEX TO WORDS, PHRASES AND SENTENCES

157

T